THE MAD SAILOR OF PETERSFIELD

DAVID GREEN

Published by Hastings Press 2022
ISBN: 978-1-904109-38-9
Printed in Poland by Booksfactory

www.hastingspress.co.uk

Contents

Preface	1
1. 'Strange out-of the-world place'	3
2. 'Crazy sailor runs amok'	11
3. 'Fatal shot'	21
4. 'Downright murder'	35
5. 'Tales of demonology'	49
6. Committal hearing	63
7. The Trial	69
8. 'His Majesty's Pleasure Man'	77
Afterword	89
Appendix I Herbert Mitchell's Statement	97
Appendix II 'How I Escaped from a Lunatic Asylum'	99
Select Bibliography	103
Acknowledgements	105
Index	107

Preface

I can't remember when I first heard the story about the mad sailor of Petersfield. I suppose it must have been in 1994, around the time I came to live in the town.

It's a simple tale. In 1906 a naval stoker called Herbert Mitchell journeys on foot from Portsmouth to Petersfield and runs amok through the town with a loaded rifle, firing indiscriminately and shooting one woman dead. He is eventually arrested, found to be insane, and locked away in Broadmoor criminal lunatic asylum for the rest of his life. A tragic case, certainly; a drama with elements of suspense and terror, undoubtedly; but hardly a murder *cause célèbre* on a par with Reg Christie of 10 Rillington Place, or the acid bath killer John George Haigh, or the Sunday school teacher Norman Thorne who dismembered and buried his sweetheart on his poultry farm in Crowborough. On the surface, the story of the mad sailor of Petersfield has little appeal for the *aficionado* of true crime. There is no great mystery to solve, no whodunit, no Gothic villain, no celebrity detective inspector working his last case. As one crime reporter described it, the residents of Petersfield were actually lucky — had the rifleman's aim been better, there might have been a massacre.

All murders are interesting but some are more interesting than others. Initially, I didn't think Herbert Mitchell, or Joseph Burbidge as he was sometimes called, was worth bothering with.

A quarter of a century passed before I turned my attention seriously to the mad sailor case. I'd just finished editing a book on the dreadful murder of Fanny Adams in Alton, and I felt I wanted a different kind of crime for my next writing project, something less harrowing but with local flavour. I remembered the case of the mad sailor of Petersfield. If nothing else, it would be interesting to write about a murder that took place only a few minutes' walk from my home. I decided to look into it a little more closely.

*

I began my research at the Portsmouth History Centre, where I found several accounts of the murder in back copies of the *Hampshire Post*. Almost from the start, I sensed that something was not quite right. Witness statements were inconsistent and contradictory. Expert testimony was flawed. Delving deeper, it seemed to me there was no reliable evidence to substantiate the charge of murder. I learned that Mitchell was actually a highly competent rifleman who could reliably hit a target at a range of 500 yards — yet according to press reports he was a dangerous felon who had apparently failed to execute a massacre because his aim was so poor. Things didn't stack up.

In 2020 I was finally able to obtain a copy of Mitchell's Broadmoor case file (medical records are closed for 100 years after a patient dies). Alongside information on Mitchell's behaviour in Broadmoor and details of his physical and mental health, the file contained a four-page statement by Mitchell giving his side of the story regards the Petersfield shooting. For the first time, we had 'the mad sailor's' version of events, and it confirmed my belief that he had been the victim of a miscarriage of justice.

After spending almost a year studying the case, I am convinced of Herbert Mitchell's innocence. I give my reasons in this book. He was wrongly condemned as a mad man and falsely accused of murder. The unfairness and inadequacy of his trial are staggering. There are villains and monsters in this book, but Herbert Mitchell is not one of them.

1

'Strange out-of-the-world place'

Tipner West is one of the last wild places along the shoreline of Portsmouth Harbour. Situated on the north-western corner of Portsea Island, it is a low-lying expanse of grass and cleared scrubland ending in saltwater marsh and mud flats. In October, flocks of wintering brent geese darken the skies above Tipner, filling the air with their calls and cries.

It has always been an isolated and rather desolate area. In the early 1800s, the Board of Ordnance began storing gunpowder on the island in windowless brick-built sheds; barracks were later added for the troops guarding the site. When Field Marshal Evelyn Wood visited the facility in 1902, he found a 'strange out-of-the-world place' where an officer, two sergeants and thirty-three men loitered around protecting ammunition worth less than £120.[1]

Between the wars the Royal Navy established one of their anti-gas defence training schools on the peninsula. Since then the site has been used for a variety of industrial purposes — as a brick factory, a tar distillery, a timber yard, and a coal depot, each activity leaving its own taint on the land. Large areas have become contaminated with asbestos. In 1955 the corpse of a baby, wrapped in a bloodstained mackintosh, washed up on the foreshore, its face mottled with curious red sores.[2] More recently the location was earmarked as an emergency no-deal Brexit lorry park for Portsmouth Harbour, and as a drive-through coronavirus testing centre.

Most of Tipner West is occupied by the 15 hectare Royal Navy firing range.[3] The ranges were completed in the 1890s and extended and widened a decade later. The berms or raised earthen embankments running horizontally across the ground have the appearance of giant burial mounds. The firing lanes are orientated slightly to the north-west to eliminate shooting into the sun. A high concrete wall at the far end of the ground behind the target line catches stray shots fired by raw recruits. For many decades the ranges were in constant use by the gunnery school on neighbouring Whale Island; matches were regularly held between teams representing the Portsmouth Rifle Club and the Royal Naval Barracks. Today, wire-mesh fencing seals off the disused range from the surrounding land. Bats roost under the M275 motorway bridge that passes over the neck of the peninsula.

*

1 Evelyn Wood, *From Midshipman to Field Marshal* (New York: E.P. Dutton & Co., 1906), pp.270-272.
2 'Baby's body on Tipnor foreshore', *Portsmouth Evening News*, 10 May 1955.
3 In 2014 the land was sold to Portsmouth City Council for development as a garden-style village consisting of 4000 new houses and a 1 million square feet marine hub.

On Monday, 13 August 1906, it was the turn of stokers from the hulked training vessel HMS *Nelson*, moored in Portsmouth dockyard, to begin their week-long musketry training at Tipner. Most of them were new to the service, with little or no experience of firearms. Each day they marched the three miles from their ship to the firing range, arriving around 9.00 in the morning. After several hours at the range, which included a break for refreshments at the musketry hall, they marched back to *Nelson* in the late afternoon. That week there were upward of 350 men, drawn from various naval establishments along the Hampshire coast, receiving training at the range.

In the first decade of the twentieth century, the British Army began overhauling its small arms training methods. Between 1899 and 1902, Britain had been at war with the South African republics of Transvaal and Orange Free State. The British Army eventually prevailed, but not before they had suffered a string of humiliating early defeats at the hands of Afrikaner farmers. Consequently, in the immediate post-Boer period, new improved Musketry Regulations were issued by the War Office,[4] and serious efforts were made to raise the general level of rifle shooting and marksmanship among serving regulars and army reservists. The new Regulations emphasised individual and independent shooting over drill. As well as being taught how to judge distance and estimate range, how to adopt correct firing posture, and how to load and fire in accordance with His Majesty's Regulations, recruits were trained in snap shooting (i.e. leaning out and firing from behind cover) rather than the traditional British assault tactic of volley firing from exposed front lines. The new methods were to prove highly effective: by the time the British Expeditionary Force sailed to France in August 1914, soldiers were routinely firing fifteen rounds a minute (the 'Mad Minute' standard), and they had a far better appreciation of the advantage of concealment under conditions of warfare. The soldiers produced from 1905 and 1906 onwards were vastly superior to the infantry that had fought in Victoria's little colonial wars.[5]

On Friday morning, around a quarter-past ten, first-class petty officer Henry Birch, the chief firearms instructor at Tipner, first realised that one of the *Nelson* stokers was missing. As the 2nd and 4th sections lined up for their first snapping exercise of the day, one of their number — Herbert Mitchell[6] — failed to answer to his muster. Earlier that morning Mitchell had asked permission to visit the latrine, and that was the last time anyone could remember seeing him.

It was a grave offence for Mitchell to absent himself without leave from his unit; it was doubly alarming that he should break away from the range with his rifle. The incident was reported to Warrant Officer Walter Rose, the gunner in overall charge at the Tipner firing camp. After searching the infantry barracks and other outbuildings, Birch walked to the nearby village of Stamshaw where he

4 H.M.S.O., *The Musketry Regulations* (London, 1905).
5 See Spencer Jones, *From Boer War to World War: Tactical Reform in the British Army 1902–1914* (University of Oklahoma Press, 2012).
6 Herbert Mitchell had enlisted in the Royal Navy in 1906 under the false name 'Joseph Burbidge'. For convenience, however, he is referred to throughout this book by his birth name.

expected to find Mitchell drinking in the Mother Shipton or the Stamshaw Arms. But there was no sign of the missing stoker. Amazingly, despite the seriousness of Mitchell's disappearance, for the next hour or so Rose and Birch did nothing, believing it was merely 'an ordinary breach of discipline' and that the sailor would come back of his own accord in time for dinner. However, when Mitchell failed to return by 12.50, Rose finally telephoned senior staff at Whale Island to report that a man had gone AWOL. Meanwhile, rather belatedly, Birch organised a search party of twenty men to go out into the scrubland and the coastal mudflats behind the sea wall.

At 2.15 Birch marched his men off the range and back to *Nelson*. It was only then, about five hours after Mitchell had first slipped away, that he was reported missing to his commanding officer.

Rather casually, the Naval authorities formed the opinion that Mitchell was still on Portsea Island somewhere; they assumed he might have made his way along Queen Street or Edinburgh Road, and was now on a pub crawl down The Hard. Certainly, they evinced no great concern over the man's disappearance, and no round-up patrols were despatched from the ships.

In fact, on leaving the range, Mitchell had simply strolled past the Stamshaw Chemical Works, crossed the North End Recreation Ground and the allotment gardens, and headed east across the fields to the Green Posts Inn on London Road, where he turned north and followed the tramway off the island, passing through Hilsea and fording the creek at Portsea drawbridge. By the time Birch and Rose had decided what action they ought to take, he was already several miles away in the rolling Hampshire countryside.

In the days and weeks that followed, many questions would be asked about the events at Tipner. What concerned the authorities most of all was not so much that a man had walked away unnoticed from his unit, but that he had done so with his rifle and a considerable amount of ammunition.

Safety procedures were supposedly rigorously enforced at Tipner. When not being used for training purposes, firearms and live ammunition were kept securely under lock and key in the armoury. Firearms were only served out to recruits at the start of each day's training.[7] The quantity of ammunition unpacked was always kept to the minimum needed; cartridges were issued only when the shooter was in the correct firing position at a recognised firing point, and bullets were never loaded until it was the shooter's turn to fire. At the inquest, Birch described to the coroner how, after issuing cartridges, he always stamped his foot on the lid of the ammo box and kept it there until the superintendent at the range gave the order to issue ammunition to the next man. There is no reason to disbelieve Birch on this point, but his testimony comes across as slightly defensive, even desperate.

7 The service rifle in use at that time was the Lee-Metford MKII. It was Britain's first smallbore high velocity military rifle. Its most notable feature was a detachable box magazine that could be loaded with up to 10 cartridges. A 12inch double sided bayonet could be attached to the end of the muzzle. The Lee-Metford rifle was partnered with the .303 inch British service cartridge, a round-nosed lead bullet with a hard outer casing made from cupro-nickel.

According to Birch, Mitchell was issued a total of 49 rounds of ball ammunition over the four days he was at Tipner. On Tuesday he was issued seven rounds at the 200 yards firing point and a further seven rounds at the 300 yards firing point. On Wednesday he was issued seven rounds apiece at both the 500 and 600 yards firing points. On Thursday he received 21 rounds — seven for a moving ('running man') target, and fourteen for a disappearing/reappearing ('vanishing snapper') target.[8] No ammunition was issued to him on Monday or on the day he went missing.

Tuesday and Wednesday were what were known as individual firing days, when one instructor supervised two men. Consequently, it would have been impossible for Mitchell not to have fired all his rounds on those days. Similarly, on the Thursday morning, there was only one man firing at any one time at the running man target.

Realistically, the only opportunity Mitchell had to smuggle cartridges was on Thursday afternoon when up to 18 men fired all at the same time against the clock at the vanishing snapper target. During this exercise, it was certainly feasible for a man to aim his rifle but not fire it, unload his weapon without being noticed, and hide the bullets in his trouser pockets. The men were never personally searched until they left the range and then only their pouches were frisked — never their pockets or their coats.

When questioned by the coroner, Birch admitted that Mitchell had hit the vanishing man target four times. This meant that Mitchell could only have smuggled at the most ten cartridges from the range. Yet we know for certain that more than three times that number of rounds was subsequently fired by Mitchell on Friday afternoon, and by his own account Mitchell claimed to have smuggled between 30 and 40 rounds from the Tipner supply.[9] How he managed to procure so much ammunition is a mystery: possibly he could have persuaded one or two of his comrades to do the same as he had done and smuggle bullets during the Thursday afternoon class firing;[10] alternatively, the discipline and safety precautions at Tipner may not have been quite as rigorous as Birch asserted.

At any rate, what seems to have happened is that somehow, over the course of the week's training, Mitchell got his hands on perhaps as many as 30 rounds; he turned up at the range on Friday morning, took possession of his rifle, nipped to the latrine, and covertly made off across the fields. In his own words, he simply 'strolled away from the rifle range'.[11] He was a big, strong, healthy man, dressed in full Navy uniform with leggings and cap; in his arms he carried his Lee-Metford service rifle. Over his shoulder, slung sash-wise, was a bandolier containing enough ammunition for a massacre.

8 Vanishing man targets appeared randomly for only a second or so before disappearing again.
9 D/H14/02/2/1/2157. Statement from Herbert C. J. Mitchell to Superintendent Brayn, 7 May 1907.
10 In 1905 there had been a series of riots by stokers at Portsmouth. The courts martial of eleven men took place in November 1906, but a poisonous, near-mutinous mood pervaded the dockyard for at least twelve months prior to that – fertile ground, one might imagine, for infractions such as stealing ammunition from the firing range.
11 D/H14/02/2/1/2157. Statement from Herbert C. J. Mitchell to Superintendent Brayn, 7 May 1907.

*

On leaving Portsea Island, Mitchell found himself in open countryside. To the east, as far as the eye could see, vast cornfields and untrimmed hedges stretched away into the distance. He could just make out the grandstands and perimeter fences of Farlington racecourse. To the west, ponds and meadows turned gradually into an endless succession of saltings and mudflats. Trails of mist floated over the reeds and high grasses. Here and there pieces of agricultural machinery – a potato riddle, the wheel from a swath turner – lay abandoned in the fields beside the road. Mitchell rested for a moment, weighing up his options. Ahead, about a mile or so north, was the small town of Cosham, nestling at the foot of the long chalk ridge of Portsdown Hill. Along the crest were a series of red-brick forts built in the 1860s to guard Portsea Island from landward attack. Mitchell continued northwards, crossing the railway line at Cosham and passing through the town.

The Portsdown and Horndean Light Railway ran a tram service alongside the London Road connecting Cosham with Horndean. Up until 1903, when the line was electrified, teams of ponies used to pull the carriages up the slope and along the tramway. The tramcars were painted green and white, and they took 20 minutes to cover the six mile journey. Mitchell probably didn't take the tram; he will have walked up the hill by the roadside. It was a cosy little world at the top of Portsdown Hill, with the George Inn getting ready for the lunchtime trade and Sparks' tea gardens serving iced barley water and cake in the morning sunshine. The waitresses wore uniforms that exactly matched the doilies and napkins laid out on the tabletops. Most days and always at the weekend a brass band entertained the visitors. From the brow of the hill, Mitchell will have looked back at the way he had come, marvelling at the extensive views of Portsmouth and its harbour, the rifle range at Tipner, the Solent and the Isle of Wight in the distance.

The railway continued down the slope to Horndean, trundling through the fields and hedgerows bright with woodbine and wild roses. The ancient Forest of Bere once covered most of the land in this part of south-east Hampshire. By the turn of the twentieth century, however, the landscape had been worked into a mix of lowland heath, wooded pasture, and small grassy paddocks that nonetheless retained the character of a medieval hunting forest. Small villages were dotted about, connected by narrow lanes and bridleways. Mitchell resumed his journey along the London Road, being overtaken at intervals by the little tram as it shuttled back and forth. Many times he stopped at the edge of the woods, dazzled by the beauty of the sun as it burst through the canopy of trees. He passed through Purbrook and half an hour later arrived at Waterlooville. Just off the main street was Sydenham House, a small school catering for children found living in brothels or wandering without proper guardianship. Mitchell had family in Sydenham, and the name of the establishment will have chimed with him. As he skirted the property he noticed three little girls in the front garden, aged no more than eight, sitting fully-clothed in a tin bath propped on brick supports. They were drinking pretend cups of tea. Silently, they observed

Mitchell as he walked by, their teacups raised halfway to their mouths. Cowplain was the next village, and then, at around midday, he reached the terminus of the Light Railway at Horndean and Crookley.

*

Mitchell had no idea where he was heading. Although he'd been born in the Test Valley and may have grown up there, he had never really been out and about in the Hampshire countryside before, apart from on military exercises. He was simply following the main road wherever it took him. Other than the Gosport Ferry and the steamer service linking Eastney Barracks with Hayling Island, and of course the railway line, there was only one way off Portsea Island, and that was via the London Road where it crossed the drawbridge over the creek at Hilsea. Today the route from London to Portsmouth follows the A3 trunk road, but back in 1906 the road was little more than a country lane, and in places barely that. Anyone travelling north from Portsmouth eventually ended up at Cosham and Horndean. If the Naval authorities had had their wits about them, and despatched a cycle patrol along the London Road, they would have detected Mitchell's whereabouts within minutes. After all, he was not skulking behind the hedgerows or trying to lie low; he was striding confidently along the main road beside the tramline in full military costume with a rifle in his arms. In fact, he would have presented quite a conspicuous figure, and based on the number of children who waved at him as the tram clattered by, it was obvious his presence was arousing considerable curiosity. Of course, given the proximity of the great naval base at Portsmouth, it was not unusual for sailors, singly or in small parties, armed or unarmed, to be seen roaming around the villages and neighbouring hills at all hours of the day. Military manoeuvres were constantly in operation and troops were forever on the move. No doubt this circumstance partly explains why Mitchell's presence on the road leading out of Portsmouth did not trigger any sense of alarm in the public or excite the attention of local police forces. The *Hampshire Post* inaccurately described him as possessing 'the maniac, wild, glaring eyes, dishevelled hair, and the attitude of a hunted man';[12] but in fact, people he met along the way thought him a friendly normal-looking young chap going about his perfectly lawful business. He presented no outward signs of mental turmoil or frenzy. He bore no intense, reptile-like 'dead stare' that is said to characterise the visage of rampage killers on a mission.

According to his own account, and really it is the only account we have of the first part of his journey, he met a 'respectable tramp' on the road and went drinking with him, possibly in the Spotted Cow in Cowplain. They shared several drinks, Mitchell paying for them both, before saying their goodbyes and going their separate ways.[13]

*

12 *Hampshire Post*, 24 August 1906.
13 D/H14/02/2/1/2157. Statement from Herbert C. J. Mitchell to Superintendent Brayn, 7 May 1907.

Beyond Horndean, the landscape took on a more barren and remote aspect. The beech and conifer woodlands gave way to the undulations of the chalk downs. The hillsides were covered with short grass and patches of gorse. Just discernible on the ridge to the east were the remains of Chalton windmill. The noise of lime-burners working away at their excavations in the quarries further north carried down into the valley. Ahead lay Butser Hill, the highest point in Hampshire, and a little way beyond that, in its lee, the small town of Petersfield. Mitchell met hardly anyone on this leg of his journey, just the occasional cyclist or tradesman on horseback.

About three miles beyond Horndean, close to the Hogs Lodge Inn, Mitchell encountered a small party of mounted infantry. They were sitting in a field, drinking whiskey from a bottle. There were military manoeuvres taking place that afternoon over at Woolmer Forest camp on the other side of Petersfield; perhaps the soldiers had come from there. In spite of their rowdiness and raucous singing, they seemed friendly enough. After a few greetings they invited Mitchell to share their liquor. He climbed over the gate and sat with them for a while. As well as whiskey they had as a curious licorice-flavoured spirit in a tall blue bottle. Mitchell reckoned he spent half an hour or so with the soldiers.[14]

We know it was around this time that Mitchell lost his cap.[15] Perhaps one of the soldiers playfully swiped it off his head, throwing it to his mates when Mitchell lunged to grab it back. What may have begun as good-natured joshing soon turned into something a little crueller. Tiring of it, Mitchell left the men and continued on his way. Possibly Mitchell was a little sozzled at this point, although certainly he wasn't drunk. If anything, the alcohol had brought on a rather sour, resentful edge to his humour: he was annoyed at being teased by the Woolmer soldiers, and disgruntled at the loss of his cap.

In a short while he came to the Coach and Horses at a place called Gravel Hill. He would have liked to stop here for another drink — the pub's dark interior and the sound of men's laughter from inside was suddenly very appealing — but his money was all gone. He regretted now frittering it away on that tramp a few miles back. The road was a little steeper here. A milestone told him he was sixty miles from London, thirteen from Portsmouth, and four from Petersfield. The road divided, one branch forking north-east over the downs in the direction of Buriton, the other continuing northwards on to Petersfield.

Mitchell was still deciding which route to take when a soldier rode up behind him on a bicycle. He may have belonged to the same troop of men drinking in the field near the Hogs Lodge turnoff; he may even have been sent back by them to aggravate Mitchell further. Waving his carbine in the air, he ordered Mitchell to surrender his arms and ammunition. But Mitchell saw that the soldier's weapon was not loaded: he raised his own rifle and fired a warning shot over the man's head. The soldier quickly jumped onto his bicycle and beat a hasty

14 Op cit.
15 The cap was later found the same day by a farmer. See *Hants and Sussex News*, 22 August 1906.

retreat, pedalling down the road as fast as he could. In a spirit of triumphalism, Mitchell fired two further shots into the air.

Clearly, Mitchell had not wanted to injure the soldier; he intended only to scare him off. But it was an exceedingly reckless act to discharge a firearm on the street like that. It showed wanton disregard for the safety of the public. He could not have known what was beyond the target and in the line of fire. In fact, the first bullet whipped through a stand of trees beside the road and travelled almost 200 yards before striking the bedsheets flapping on the clothesline in the garden of Bottom Cottage. At the time Mrs Susan Blackman was pegging out her weekly wash. Luckily, the bullet missed her by twenty feet or so. Startled, she hurried indoors. Her husband heard the gunshots and went out into the road to investigate. Allan Blackman was the game keeper and head warrener for the Buriton Manor Estate. In his own way he was used to massacres: twice a month between October and February an average of 600 rabbits were culled on the Manor estate: afterwards, he liked to lay out their small bloodied bodies on trestle tables in the beer garden at the Coach and Horses as if they were desserts to match the raspberry cream horns on sale at Sparks' tea gardens. For a laugh he sometimes went out shooting rabbits on Watership Down.[16]

Blackman confronted Mitchell and there were sharp words on both sides. Mitchell advised the game keeper to keep his nose out of it. 'I am going to shoot a soldier,' he said, matter-of-factly. Astonishingly, given Mr Blackman's professional knowledge of guns and sporting rifles, he didn't seem to notice that Mitchell was wearing a bandolier packed with ammunition. 'You've got nothing to shoot with,' he told Mitchell. 'Oh yes I have!' came the reply, and he puffed his chest out proudly like a hotel commissionaire.[17]

Mitchell chose the northerly track and strode off once more into the hills. He was staggered by the grandeur of the landscape, the views on all sides as the chalk gorge cut through the hill-top. He felt bounteous, euphoric almost. He knew now where he was heading — to Petersfield. He didn't know anything about the town, its history or its character; he didn't know anyone who lived there, and he had no money for food or shelter. But this didn't concern him in the slightest. He was convinced he would never see the Portsmouth dockyard again. In some deep, almost magical way, he felt his destiny was approaching and that his passage upon the Earth was reaching its apocalyptic climax.

16 Of course, this was many decades before Richard Adams wrote *Watership Down*, his famous children's novel about rabbits. Information from Buriton Heritage website, see buriton.org.uk/history/local-pheasant-and-rabbit-shoots

17 *Hampshire Chronicle*, 25 August 1906.

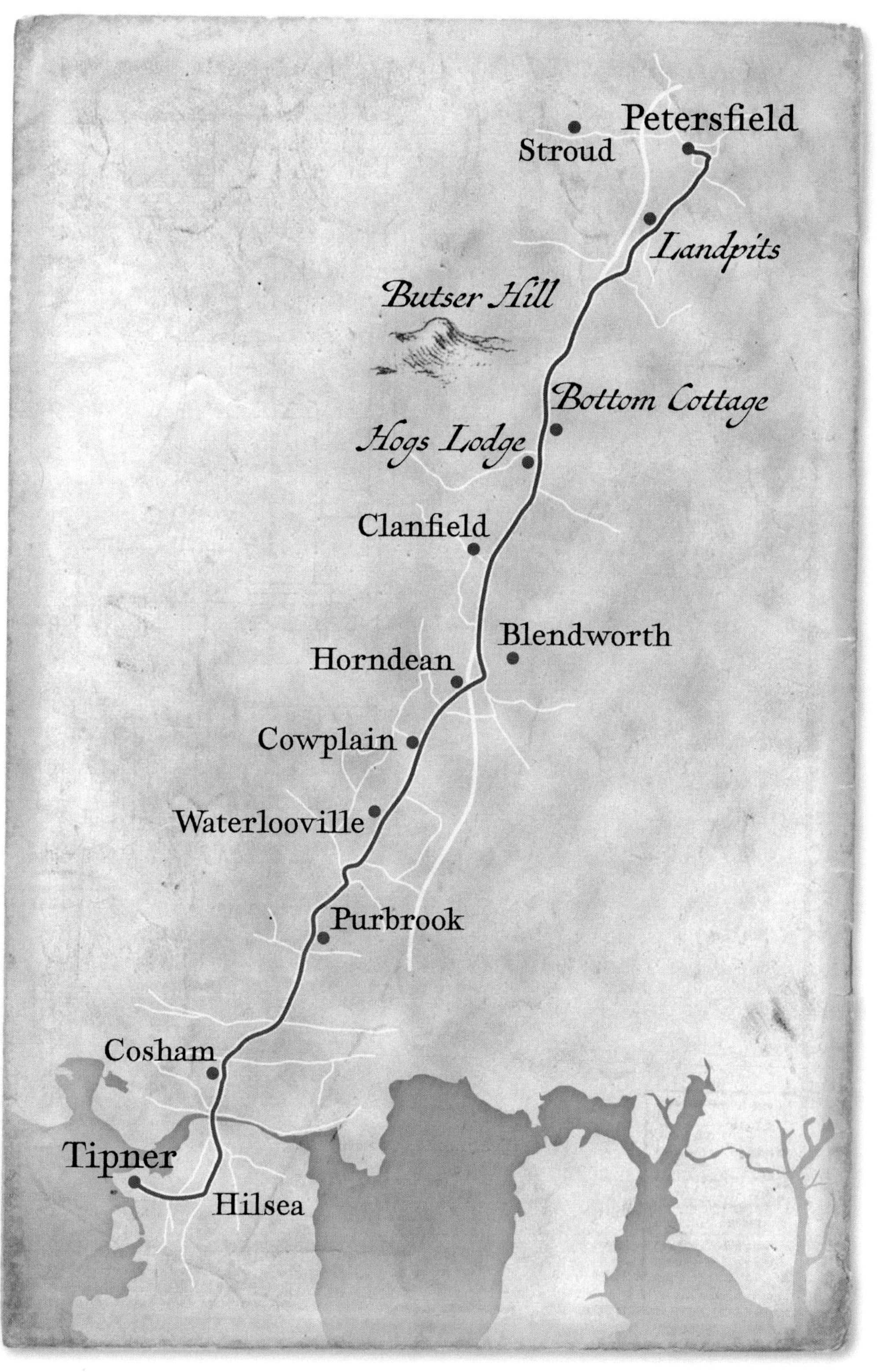

1. Mitchell's route across Hampshire

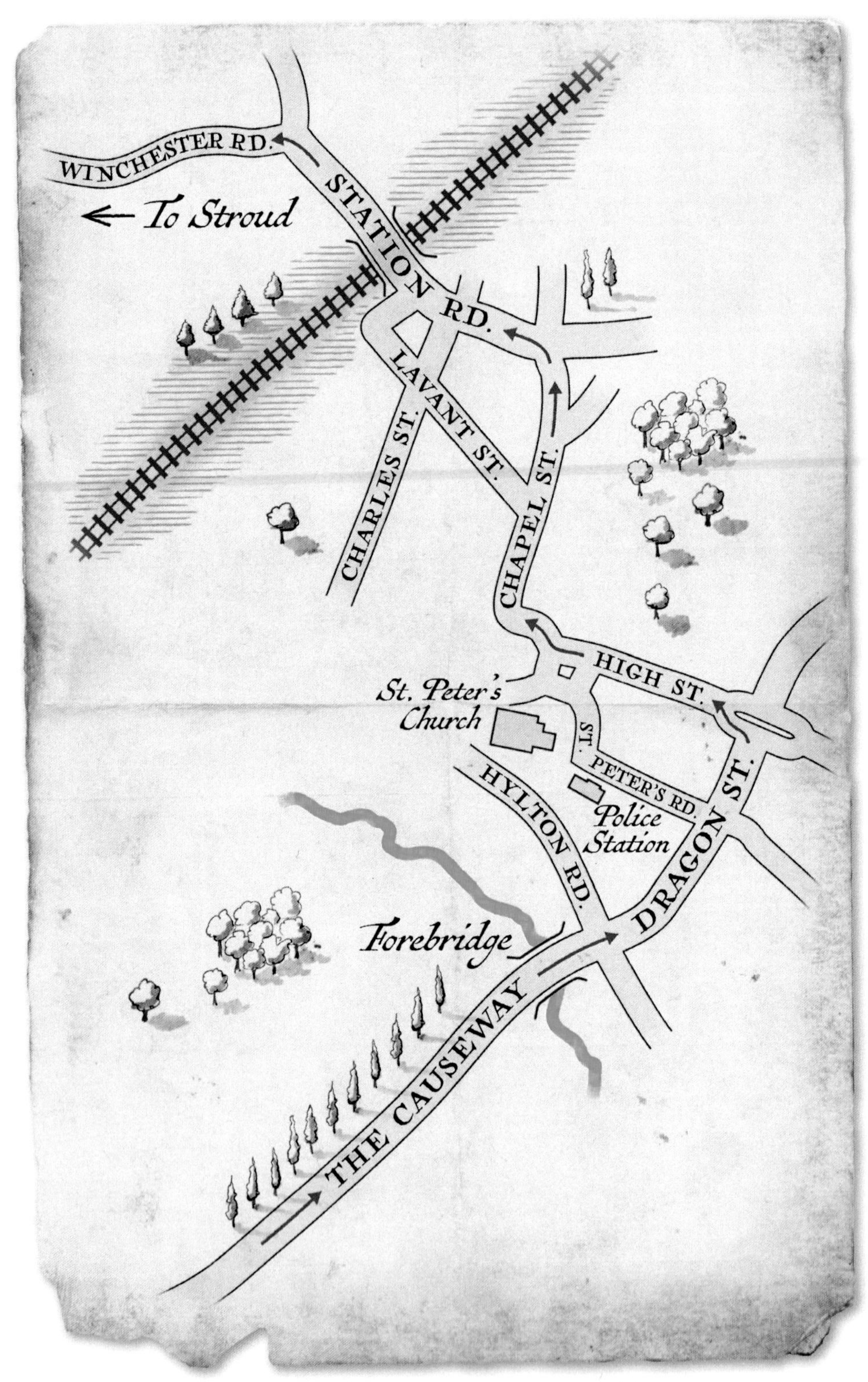

2. Mitchell's route through Petersfield

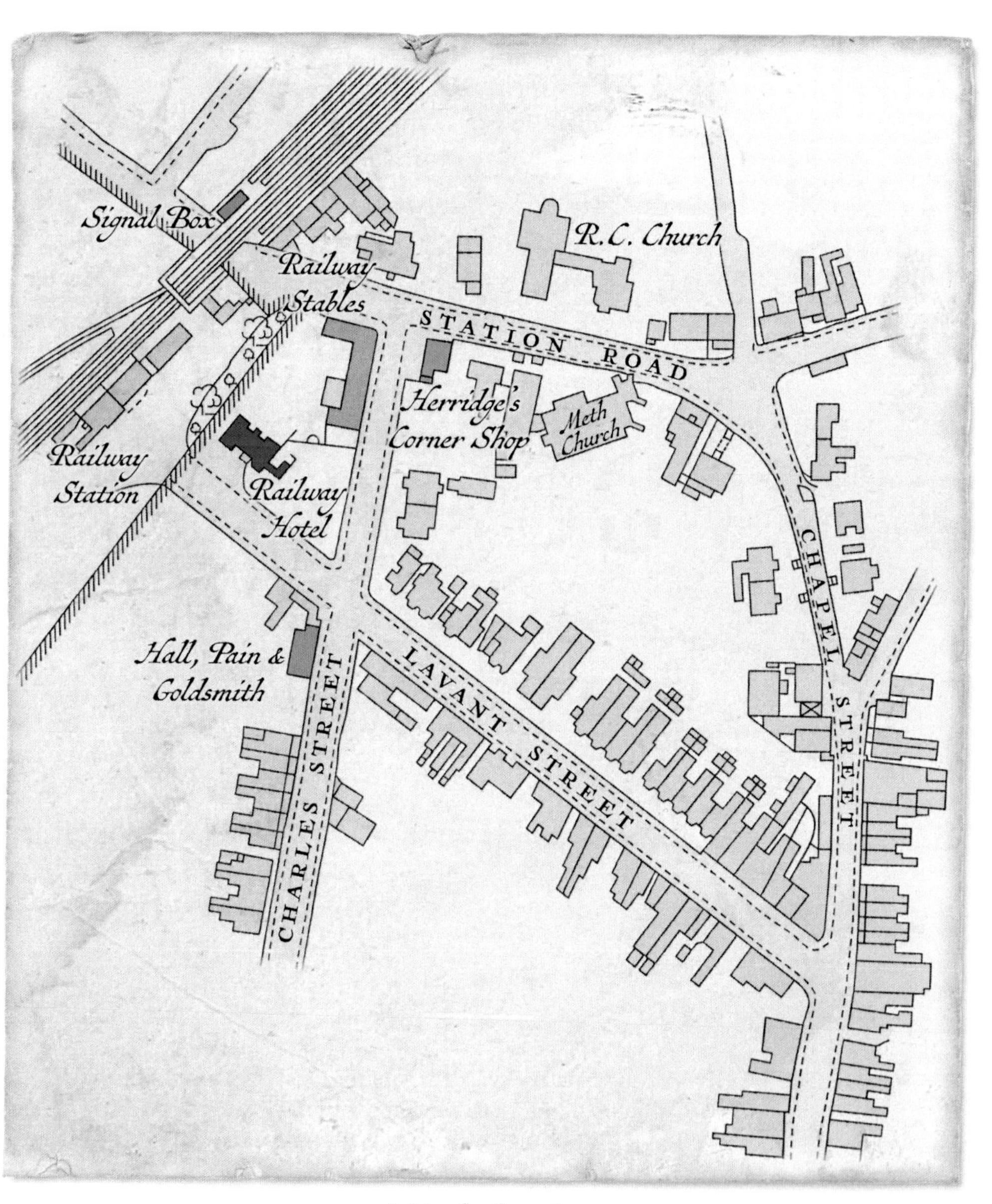

3. Murder location

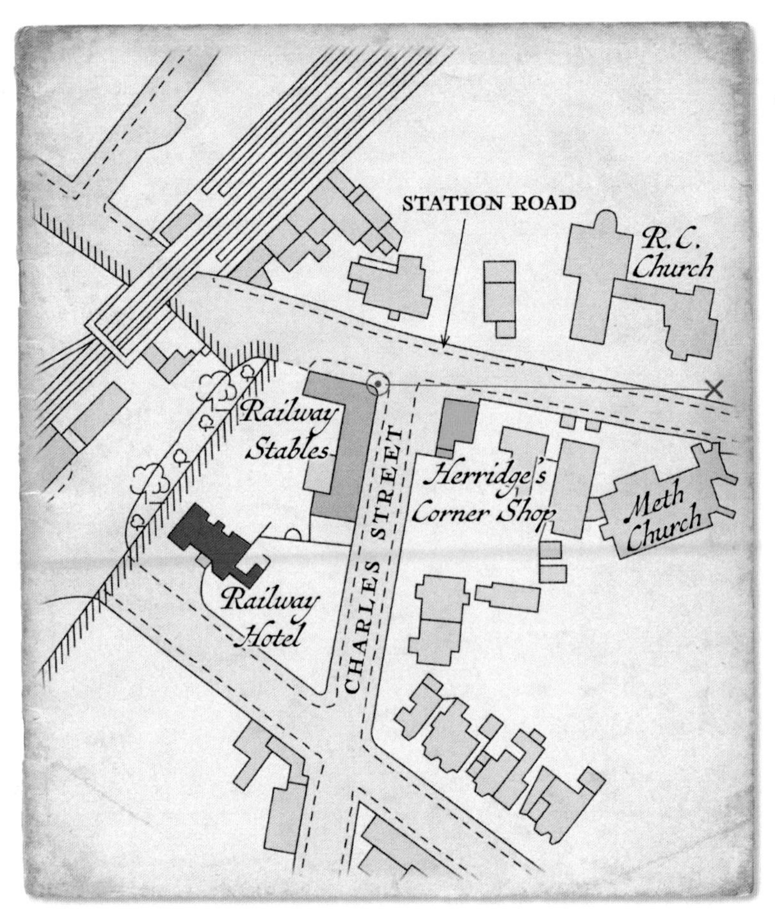

4. Murder location (detail). 'X' marks the position of the gunman, and the red line shows the trajectory of the bullet

5. View of murder scene today. *Courtesy of Tim Coel and Hülle Architecture and Design*

2

'Crazy sailor runs amok'

News of the shooting incident travelled quickly. Once Mitchell had left the scene Mrs Blackman rushed out into the street and told everyone she met about the bullet that had struck her clothesline. Breathlessly, she went into the Coach and Horses and regaled all the regulars with her dramatic account of the armed sailor on a mission to shoot a soldier.

At this point Mr Douglas Fleet Goldsmith makes his first appearance in our story. Still a relatively young man in his late twenties, he was a partner at the auctioneering, surveyors and estate agents firm of Hall, Pain and Goldsmith, working out of their newly-opened Petersfield branch on the corner of Lavant Street and Charles Street.[18] Mostly, he handled the sale of livestock, farm vehicles and utensils – sheep, pigs and calves, iron dung carts, hay-making machines, milk churns and so on. In the days ahead, the press would do their best to depict Mr Goldsmith as the hero of the hour. The truth is, though, that he was a deeply unpleasant and depraved individual.

That Friday afternoon he was riding home to Blendworth Farm on horseback along the London Road. He actually passed Mitchell near Bolinge Hill Lane where the road crossed the railway line at Mapledurham. The man was sitting beside the road, holding his rifle between his knees, but Goldsmith scarcely gave him a second glance. Now, on reaching Gravel Hill, he sensed a commotion and asked a road mender called Albert Cook[19] what was going on. He loved speaking down from the saddle to the common working man, barking out orders and peremptory demands. Mrs Blackman had already spoken to Cook, and Cook relayed much the same account to Goldsmith. Recalling the sailor he had passed on the road about a mile and a half back, he instantly turned his horse round and rode off the way he had come. Goldsmith had a grandiose sense of his own importance and he sensed a golden opportunity to glorify himself in a public drama.

He found Mitchell lying face down on the grass verge beside the road a couple of hundred yards beyond the turn off for Landpits. He had adopted the prone firing position as taught at Tipner earlier in the week, his rifle gripped ready for shooting. So far as we can tell he was aiming his rifle at a cluster of dwellings almost four hundred yards away on the left hand side of the road opposite Causeway Farm, although why he should target these specific buildings isn't clear. The area was known as Brickfields on account of the large brick and tile works (Larcombe's) nearby; perhaps they were simply the first group of domestic dwellings Mitchell had encountered since leaving Horndean.

18 Estate agents Jacobs and Hunt occupy the premises today. See 'Jacobs and Hunt Centenary', *Bulletin Petersfield Area Historical Society*, Vol. 4, No. 10 (Autumn 1995), p.12.
19 Cook was forty-three and lived at 19 Windsor Road in Petersfield.

In his interviews with the newspapers and during his testimony at court, Goldsmith offered conflicting statements about what had happened at Landpits. At first, he claimed Mitchell had shot at him as he rode past. According to this version Goldsmith leapt off his horse to take cover behind a tree, and the riderless animal bolted across the fields. Somehow Goldsmith recaptured his mount and rode hard into Petersfield, all the while dodging a hail of bullets fired by Mitchell.[20] Of course, this was pure fantasy, something out of Buffalo Bill's Wild West Show. Later, under oath at the magistrates' hearing, Goldsmith simply claimed he had ridden past Mitchell without incident and didn't stop till he reached the town police station, where he gave information on the sailor's whereabouts to Superintendent King. But this second version isn't true either. There is a third account from Mitchell himself. According to Mitchell, Goldsmith pulled up beside him as he was lying on the grass verge and tried to trample him with his horse. Desperately, Mitchell rolled onto his back, trying to avoid the stomping hooves by squeezing into the hedgerow. He fired a warning shot into the air to frighten the horseman. It did the trick – spitting abuse at the sailor, Goldsmith rode off at speed towards Petersfield.[21]

Alfred Etherington, a nine-year-old boy, was playing nearby on his bicycle.[22] He heard the gunshot and, thinking Mitchell was on manoeuvres, came over and asked the sailor if there were more troops on the way. At first Mitchell ignored him, but when the boy started cycling off he called out to him, asking if the lad had any cigarettes. Something in Mitchell's manner alarmed the boy, impelling him to hurry away.

Still lying by the side of the road, Mitchell was passed by Lance-Corporal White of the 2nd South Lancashire Regiment as he cycled into Petersfield.[23] Stationed at Blackdown Barracks near Camberley, he was out for the afternoon on pass, exploring the Hampshire countryside. Mitchell, however, seems to have assumed that White was in cahoots with the dragoon who had accosted him earlier at Gravel Hill, for he shot at the hind wheel of the soldier's bicycle, shattering the rim and bursting the tyre. White dismounted and angrily came up to Mitchell, demanding to know what was going on. Barely registering the other man's presence, Mitchell calmly pointed at his rifle and fired a couple more shots down the road. Sensibly, White didn't stay to argue; he quickly picked up his damaged machine and headed off in the direction of Petersfield. A little further down the road he managed to cadge a lift from a cart driver, who ferried him and his bicycle into town.

Mitchell got up and continued on his way. Four bullet casings would later be found in the grass beside the road, marking Mitchell's exploits at Landpits. It was around a quarter past four. The late afternoon sun was breaking through the mist over Butser Hill. Mitchell had now reached the outskirts of Petersfield;

20 *Hampshire Post*, 24 August 1906.
21 D/H14/02/2/1/2157. Statement made by Herbert C. J. Mitchell to Superintendent Brayn, 7 May 1907.
22 He lived at 24 The Spain, in Petersfield, with his aunt and widowed grandmother.
23 According to Mitchell's Broadmoor statement, the soldier 'came up from the opposite direction'. D/H14/02/2/1/2157. Statement made by Herbert C. J. Mitchell to Superintendent Brayn, 7 May 1907.

he was a mile or so from the town centre, walking along The Causeway (actually the old London to Portsmouth turnpike road), which bounded the south-east corner of the town. He approached the group of dwellings at Brickfields. Among them stood a five-roomed cottage lying only a few feet back from the road in a tiny front garden.[24] He appraised the damage to the front door caused by one of his bullets. The present occupiers were a newly-married couple, Mr and Mrs Steel or Steele. At the time, Mrs Steel had been sitting at a table in her sitting room, writing a letter. She screamed as the bullet shattered the front door and ricocheted around the room, striking the front of the fireplace and just missing the back of her head. The bullet came to rest under a what-not. The *Hampshire Chronicle* continues the incident:

> She was naturally much frightened, and ran outdoors to see what the matter was, but could see no one in the road. She spoke to Mr Ben Knight, who has a builder's shop close by, and they were discussing the possibility of one of the soldiers on manoeuvres having fired the shot when the sailor came down the road . . . Mrs Steel ran indoors, and locked herself in, and in great agitation of mind watched the sailor through her sitting room window whilst he stood in the road for a few seconds looking intently at the house. To her relief he passed on.[25]

Mitchell carried on down the hill, passing the Jolly Sailor pub on his left.[26] Perhaps he chuckled at the name.

By this time Douglas Fleet Goldsmith had alerted the town police to the threat posed by the approaching gunman. He spoke to Superintendent John King, who occupied living quarters above the station with his wife and family. But the initial police response was listless and dithering. It fell to Goldsmith to take decisive action. He rode back to The Causeway, where he found Lance-Corporal White nursing his disabled bicycle. The two men conferred. They could see Mitchell further up the road, coming towards them. Mitchell spotted Goldsmith at the same time. Recognising him as the maniac who had urged his horse to trample him to the ground, Mitchell levelled his rifle. Goldsmith jumped off his mount in a swirl of cape, steered it to safety in the lane next to Mr Smart's dairy, and for some reason vaulted the hedge into the adjoining meadow beside the river. Crouched over, he made his way awkwardly alongside the hedge, rising at intervals to check on Mitchell's position. Onlookers were beginning to gather on the Forebridge, watching the sailor as he approached the town. Goldsmith waved his arms about wildly, trying to warn the crowd of the peril they faced.

If he'd wanted to, Mitchell could quite easily have put a bullet in the auctioneer's head. Popping up and down behind the hedge, he resembled one of

24 The cottage still stands today as 139 The Causeway. Back in 1906 it was numbered 3 The Causeway.
25 *Hampshire Chronicle*, 25 August 1906. Mr Ben Knight was 49; he lived at 10 St Peter's Road, Petersfield.
26 The Jolly Sailor closed in 2004 and was demolished six years later.

those disappearing/reappearing snapper figures, made of tin, deployed during target practice at Tipner rifle range.

A wagon loaded with bales of straw pulled up near the entrance to the Grange farmhouse. Mitchell dropped to one knee and shot at it, the bullet thudding into the hay. At this point, the police made their first counter move. Sergeant Joseph Allen and Constable George Pullman were the two officers selected for this sortie. They crossed over the bridge and advanced cautiously towards Mitchell, shouting at him to put his weapon down. Of course, he took no notice at all and fired into the air. The policemen scarpered up Hylton Road, hiding in the passageway between some cottages next to the gas works. They hoped Mitchell might also turn up Hylton Road, allowing them to pounce on him unawares, but Mitchell saw them poking their heads out and marched straight past the turning and up the hill into Dragon Street. The crowd scattered before him.

A hue and cry was now in progress. Mitchell broke into a run, followed at a 'safe distance' by the police.[27] When he reached Henry Gander's meat and poultry shop he dropped down on one knee again and fired in the direction of his pursuers. The bullet ricocheted off the roof of Frank and Elizabeth Newman's cottage at 32 Dragon Street, dislodging several tiles. Ann Enves, the barmaid at the Sun Inn, stepped back from the pub doorway just in time as the bullet zipped passed her. A second shot, fired in the opposite direction, sailed over the garden wall of Dr Robert Cross's surgery at 2 Dragon Street, whizzed through the branches of a mulberry tree in the centre of his lawn, before shattering a window in the Urban Council offices in Heath Road.

Alarm gripped the town. Pedestrians scampered out of the way as the sailor turned left and advanced up the High Street. In no apparent rush, Mitchell sat down on the steps of Winton House, under the massive Doric porch, training his weapon on anyone who showed themselves round the corner by the Dolphin Hotel.[28]

While this was going on, the police had re-grouped in the station forecourt. It was time for their second counterattack. Superintendent King had now taken personal command and was urging his men forward along the alley that connected St Peter's Street with the High Street. The passageway ran beside the printing works of Arthur Childs, proprietor of the *Hampshire Post*, and came out, via a wooden gate, almost exactly opposite Winton House where Mitchell was resting. The police gingerly prised opened the gate, immediately saw Mitchell sitting across the road pointing his rifle at them, and wisely retreated, shutting

27 F.G. Standfield notes '. . . it is hard to understand how onlookers were sufficiently foolish to follow "at a safe distance", as the papers put it, since a service rifle is lethal at ranges of a mile or more.' F.G. Standfield, *A History of East Meon* (Chichester: Phillimore & Co. Ltd, 1984), p.110. In fact, a report in the *British Medical Journal* describes a fatal shot from the Lee-Metford rifle at a range of between three and four miles: see 'Effects of the Lee Metford Rifle', *British Medical Journal*, Vol. 2, No. 1974 (29 October, 1898), p.1362.

28 The Dolphin was situated on the corner of Dragon Street and the High Street, where Dolphin Court stands today. It was demolished in 1965. Winton House was the residence and surgery of Dr William Panckridge. Pepys is reputed to have played bowls in the garden at the rear of the house.

the gate after them and scuttling back up the passage. The counter offensive was over.

Mitchell resumed his way up the High Street. As he passed the offices of Shield and Mackarness, solicitors, he waved his rifle in the face of sixteen-year-old Stanley Johnson, who had just stepped outside to investigate the commotion.[29] Reaching the market square, he noticed it was coming up to twenty-five to five by the church tower clock.

Following the S bend in the road he entered Chapel Street. A large flock of townsfolk still tailed his progress through the town, keeping a distance of perhaps thirty or forty yards. Several times Mitchell swung round and aimed his rifle at them, seemingly enjoying the way they gasped and scattered into nearby shops and buildings. Yet at the same time, other pedestrians and shoppers, apparently oblivious of the dangerous situation, were strolling around town on their usual everyday business. Continuing up the street, he brandished his rifle at William Hobbs standing outside his father's smithy;[30] a little further on, he confronted sixty-year-old Joseph Gard, who was leaning against the half-open gate of his builder's and decorator's yard at number 18. The *Hampshire Chronicle* described their extraordinary encounter:

> Going up to him [Mitchell] told him to stand back as he was too near for him to shoot him. Mr Gard did not budge, but stared fixedly at the man, who walked round him within a yard or two of him still pointing his rifle at him, and then crossed to the opposite side of the road and took aim. Mr Gard took shelter behind the gate post, not daring to turn and run, and the man then fortunately walked away.[31]

He turned left at the crossroads into Station Road. On the north side of the street stood the Roman Catholic church of St Laurence with its distinctive octagonal copper dome. Up ahead, just round a slight bend in the road, Mitchell could see the railway line, the signal box, and the level crossing.

Meanwhile, back at the Grange, Douglas Fleet Goldsmith had extricated himself from the meadow. The trousers of his grey suit were splashed with mud; he was beginning to sweat horribly from the unaccustomed exertion. Nonetheless, he raced across town, anxious to keep on top of the unfolding drama. Learning that the gunman was making his way along Station Road, Goldsmith sprinted up Lavant Street and turned right into Charles Street, hoping to intercept the man before he reached the railway station. When he arrived at the bottom corner of Charles Street where it joined with Station Road, he spotted Mitchell crossing the road outside the Catholic church, wielding his rifle. He noticed, too, a second man walking unconcernedly past the Methodist church on the opposite side of the road. Clearly, he hadn't seen the sailor. Goldsmith shouted out a warning,

29 'Petersfield's Day of Terror', *Bulletin Petersfield Area Historical Society*, Vol.1, No.8 (Autumn 1978), no page numbers.
30 Greggs' bakery today.
31 *Hampshire Chronicle*, 25 August 1906.

and the man — Charles Hill was his name[32] — dashed into the front garden of a neighbouring house, and took cover as best he could behind the gateway. Goldsmith himself retreated back down Charles Street, out of the line of fire. Also fleeing the scene was a dog, spooked by the atmosphere of menace; it howled as if injured by a bullet, and bolted down Charles Street at the heels of Goldsmith.

Mitchell raised his rifle.

*

The railway came to Petersfield in 1856. One of the first establishments to prosper from the expansion of the town and the influx of new visitors was the Railway Hotel. It stood outside the station entrance at 41 Lavant Street.[33] Behind the hotel was a large garden and stabling area where customers could hire transport for their onward journey — open and covered traps, broughams, brakes, waggonettes, landaus, and victorias, even dog carts. Every December, pigs, geese, sheep, and other livestock specially fatted for the Christmas market, huddled in the yard of the Railway Hotel, waiting to be sold at auction.

The landlord in 1906 was William Goble, who had taken over the business twelve months earlier when the former proprietor, Edwin Rufus, committed suicide at his home in Southsea, shooting himself with the revolver he kept under his bed for fear of burglars. On the death of Rufus, the stabling part of the business had been sublet by the land agents Messrs W & R Luker to Mr Albert Clarke of Steep.

That Friday afternoon, Margaret Treble (*née* Edwards) and her sister-in-law Amelia Maud Treble were visiting Petersfield. Margaret was thirty-six and the wife of Robert Tucker Treble, a saddle and harness maker from Lymington. Amelia's brother, Ralph, a school teacher, had driven them into town from his parents' home, Peake Farm, in East Meon. They arrived in town at approximately half-past two. Leaving the horse and trap in the stable yard behind the Railway Hotel, Ralph went off to attend to some business on the Heath, while the two ladies sauntered into town and enjoyed afternoon tea at the Coffee Tavern next to the George Hotel in The Square. Afterwards, they passed the time shop-window gazing. With them was Margaret's two-year-old daughter, Doris May.[34]

At half-past four Margaret and Amelia began making their way back to the Railway Hotel. There was some disturbance in town — a crowd was gathering at the bottom of the High Street — although they didn't know what the fuss was about. They met up with Ralph in Lavant Street. He went ahead to prepare the horse and trap for their return journey, while the two women continued walking along Charles Street, little Doris swinging on their arms between them.

32 Mr Charles R Hill (35), a bank cashier at the London and Counties bank. He lived in Rushes Road.
33 The hotel originally stood to the east of the station on the north side of Station Road, but by the 1860s it had moved to Lavant Street. See 'The Inns of Petersfield', *Petersfield Papers* (1977), pp.24-25.
34 Robert and Ralph were the sons of Thomas Tucker, an estate bailiff of Peake Farm, East Meon. Thomas was 'a man of some local status, having served as parish councillor and churchwarden'. See F.G. Standfield, *A History of East Meon*, (Chichester: Phillimore & Co. Ltd, 1984), p.8.

At around a quarter to five, just as Margaret and Amelia were turning into Station Road at the corner of the Hotel stables, a gunshot rang out. Instantly, Margaret stumbled two or three steps forward, collapsed against the stable wall, and fell to her knees on the gravel. 'A man has shot me,' she said, or words to that effect. A bullet had perforated her right thigh, passing through the muscles on the outside but not touching the bone. She was bleeding profusely, although her skirts initially concealed the extent of her injury. Amelia ran into the stable yard for help. Within seconds Ralph Treble was beside his sister-in-law. At first he thought she was merely fainting, so he called out for some brandy. Then, Albert Clarke, who had also rushed to Margaret Treble's assistance, noticed a sailor coming up the road armed with a rifle. Margaret was half-lifted and half-dragged to safety into the yard. A boy was despatched to fetch Dr Cross.

Mitchell was acting as if no one had been shot. He continued up the road, casually discharging a couple of bullets over the level crossing. He asked directions from James Herridge, who was standing in the doorway of his shop on the corner of Charles Street. The sailor appeared perfectly calm, unhurried, breathing normally. In fact, he was so cool-headed and self-controlled Herridge didn't even realise a woman had been shot just across the road. He thought Mitchell was on military manoeuvres. He explained to him that the road continued on to Winchester twenty miles away. As Mitchell headed for the level crossing, he passed the Railway stables. Alfred Clarke was inside, observing him through the window.

Reaching the other side of the crossing, Mitchell turned round once more and pointed his rifle at the police and the pursuing townsfolk. And once again, the people in the crowd ducked for cover behind walls and pressed themselves up against doorways. They saw him attach the sword bayonet to the muzzle of his rifle.

He marched on, leaving the town behind. On his left he passed the Volunteer Arms. Three minutes later he took a left fork in the road at Rushes Farm. PC Charles Stockwell, who was among the crowd trailing the sailor, described Mitchell as 'carrying his rifle like a man rabbit shooting and in readiness to fire.' A little further on Mitchell encountered Mr Fox, a hairdresser,[35] who happened to be cycling into town. Mitchell seems to have fired in the man's direction, although not with any grievous intent; the bullet ricocheted harmlessly off the ground in front of Mr Fox and landed in the hedgerow. Rather foolhardily, Mr Fox dismounted and began remonstrating with Mitchell for shooting his weapon in the public road. But there was no animosity between the men; before long Mitchell was sampling tobacco from Mr Fox's pouch, and the hairdresser had invited the good-looking sailor back to his lodgings in Rushes Road for a cup of tea. Mitchell, however, declined, suspecting an ulterior motive. 'What are you

35 He possibly assisted Mr Henry Lee, who ran a shaving, hair-cutting, and umbrella repair service from his salon at 60 Station Road. In 1911 he moved to new premises in the High Street. See Marjorie Lunt, 'Lees Hairdressers — A Family Business', *Bulletin Petersfield Area Historical Society*, No. 1 (Spring 1991), pp.20–22.

going to do with me?' asked Mitchell. 'You won't let me out again.' And then he dropped to one knee and fired at the pursuers who were just coming round the fork in the country lane. Everyone, including a couple of ladies, leapt for cover into the hedges. Mitchell carried on towards Stroud, while Mr Fox hurried off to recount his near escape to the police.

Where was Fleet Goldsmith while this was going on? He was among the party pursing Mitchell along the Winchester Road. Frustrated at the lack of decisive action by the police, who were ineffectually trailing the gunman thirty or forty yards back, Goldsmith sent a cyclist into town to fetch a double-barrel shot gun from Henry Caplen, an acquaintance of his who ran a plumbing and decorating business on the High Street.[36] Within minutes, the firearm arrived. Wasting no more time, Goldsmith vaulted over a gate on the left side of the road and began dashing across the meadows, coursing Mitchell as he headed down the Winchester Road towards Bere and Stroud. Clearly, the auctioneer was enjoying the adventure and the thrill of the chase. Goldsmith was a well known figure in Hampshire foxhunting circles — there was nothing he liked better than galloping across the downs and hangers on a frosty February afternoon on the back of his black gelding 'Paul'. But one senses he rather regretted the course his life had taken. Perhaps he had become bored by the day-to-day routines of his office job, endlessly disposing of pigs and carriage horses and dung carts. Maybe he harboured fantasies of big game hunting, running down and slaying wild animals on the Veldt, bagging buffalo and musk oxen, glorying in the butchery of the kill. Goldsmith was constitutionally unsuited to any kind of sporting endeavour requiring patience or surefootedness; he was too impetuous and lacked the nous to keep his head down in dangerous situations. Mitchell had spotted him plodding across the ploughed fields — it would have been a simple matter for him to have downed Goldsmith with a single shot to the head.

But Mitchell had run out of ammunition. He had wasted too many cartridges shooting unnecessarily into the air and aiming at shadows in the hedgerows. By the time he reached the Seven Stars Inn at Stroud he was probably thinking of turning himself over to the authorities; there was no defiance left in him, just a dull sense of acknowledgement that the adventure was coming to an end.

Inevitably, the auctioneer was waiting for him. He had positioned himself in the rear garden of a cottage seventy paces distant from the Seven Stars. He balanced his shot gun on a gate post, watching the road carefully. When Mitchell came into view, Goldsmith fired at him twice; the first shot hit him in the lumbar region (some reports say the back of the legs), the second grazed the back of his head or neck. They were both glancing blows, but they took effect. Mitchell flinched, dropped his rifle, and fell down face forwards, doubling up and rolling over. Goldsmith sprinted across the road and secured the sailor's rifle. Meanwhile, police constables Charles Stockwell and George Pullman rushed forward and

36 Caplen was also a corporal in the 3rd (Volunteer) Battalion of the Hampshire Regiment, hence his ready access to a supply of firearms.

seized the fallen man, restraining him in handcuffs and removing his boots. They manhandled him into the back of a tradesman's cart.

Goldsmith was the hero of the hour. F.G. Standfield writes in glowing terms of the auctioneer's actions:

> Even more remarkable was the courage, almost tantamount to madness, that had led Fleet Goldsmith to tackle the rifleman with a shot-gun whose effective range as a 'man-stopper' was probably no more than 60 yards. The very fact of a member of the public arming himself and acting as a one-man sheriff's posse in the year 1906 is pretty startling.[37]

A crowd of nearly a hundred people ran or cycled behind the cart as it rattled into town on its way to the police station. Constable Stockwell sat in front next to the driver Edward Fenn,[38] the military rifle lying across his knees, his chapped hands cradling it gently. Stretched out in the bed of the cart, scowling, was Mitchell, guarded by Pullman and several townspeople. A couple of other carts joined the procession. Hanging off the tailboard of one of them, shot-gun held aloft in his free hand, was the mighty Goldsmith. In a sense, the brief journey into town became a sort of mini victory parade, small boys in short cotton trousers running alongside the trucks, the crowds spilling out and lining the streets to cheer the homecoming of the conquerors. A dangerous criminal had been over-powered and brought to justice! Goldsmith soaked up the adoration.

The jubilation was short-lived, however, as later that evening news came from the Petersfield Cottage Hospital that Margaret Treble had died of her injuries.

For Mitchell, restlessly pacing up and down in his cell at St Peter's Road, it meant he would now be charged with wilful murder.

37 F.G. Standfield, *A History of East Meon*, (Chichester: Phillimore & Co. Ltd, 1984), p.10. Standfield's notes on the murder of Margaret Treble are held at the Hampshire Record Office, Ref: HRO 58M99/18.
38 Edward Fenn was the proprietor of the Dolphin Hotel stables. He was chummy with Fleet Goldsmith, being a guest at his wedding in Liss in 1908. In 1909 the Petersfield Rural District Council appointed him Inspector of Nuisances.

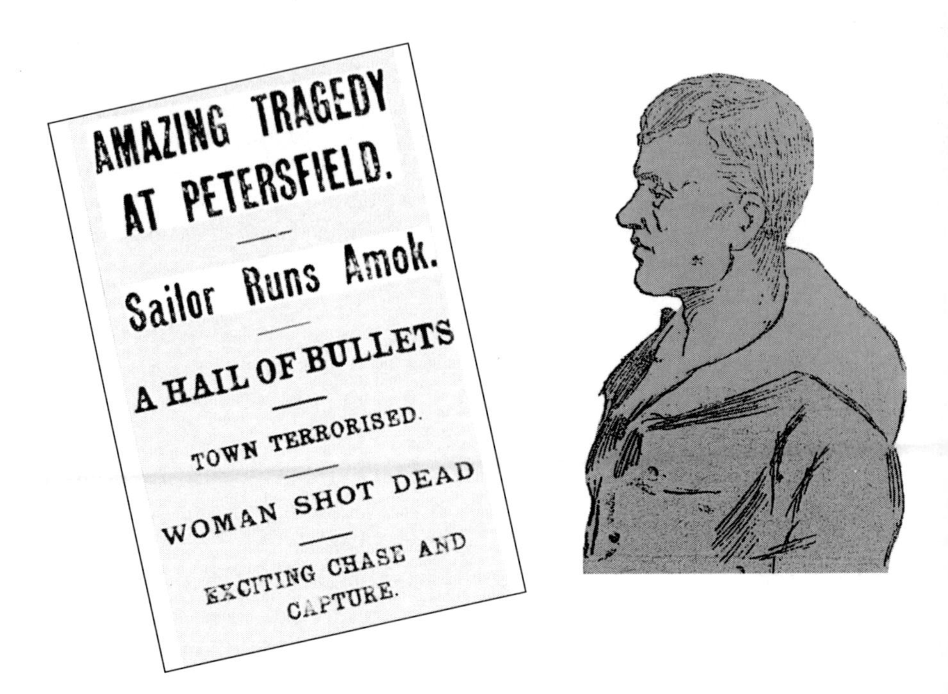
AMAZING TRAGEDY AT PETERSFIELD.

Sailor Runs Amok.

A HAIL OF BULLETS

TOWN TERRORISED.

WOMAN SHOT DEAD

EXCITING CHASE AND CAPTURE.

6. *Portsmouth Evening News,* 18 August 1906

7. Mitchell in naval gear, on the day of the shooting (*Hampshire Post*, 24 August 1906). *Copyright the British Library Board*

8. HMS *Nelson*

9. Tipner firing range. *Photo copyright Peter Facey*

10. Bottom Cottage, Gravel Hill. *Courtesy of Wilson Hill, estate agents*

11. View of Dragon Street from The Forebridge. *Provided by Petersfield Museum Limited PTFPM:2007.520*

12. High Street (south side), 1898. *Copyright the Francis Frith Collection*

13. High Street (north side), 1910. *Private collection*

14. Chapel Street (east side). *Private collection*

15. Chapel Street, 1920s. *Private collection*

16. Lavant Street leading up to railway station. *Provided by Petersfield Museum Limited PTFPM:2011.297*

17. Corner of Chapel Street and Station Road, early 20th century, showing Unsworth Cottage and St Laurence Catholic church. Mitchell turned left here. *Provided by Petersfield Museum Limited PTFPM:2007.168*

18. Station Road, 1898, showing Catholic church (without dome). Herridge's corner shop (not visible) is next to the lamp post on the left-hand pavement. *Copyright the Francis Frith collection*

19. Herridge's corner shop and Wesleyan Church, 1906. *Copyright the Francis Frith Collection*

20. The Railway Hotel, c.1970s. *Private collection*

3

'Fatal shot'

Not unexpectedly, the 'sensational shooting affair in Petersfield' became headline news in all the local newspapers:

> Never probably in the whole of its history has the town experienced a sensation of so remarkable a nature as that which, on Friday last, suddenly changed the usual tranquil appearance of the place into one of intense excitement, consternation, and alarm.[39]

Ghouls and memento hunters arrived by train to visit the scene of the tragedy. There were 'clots of blood' for them to see on the ground and on the stable walls. For a day or two scuff marks remained visible in the gravel, marking the place where the victim had fallen. Mr Herridge's corner shop did a roaring trade, selling three times the normal quantity of cake and chocolates. The day after the murder, on Saturday morning, Goldsmith turned up as usual at the Lavant Street office, but his mind wasn't on work — he spent most of the day escorting colleagues round the murder scene, crowing about his own involvement in the capture of Mitchell. At Gravel Hill, Mrs Susan Blackman was back in the Coach and Horses, repeating her own story about the stray bullet striking her washing line.

Everyone, it seemed, had a tale to tell about the rampage. Widely conflicting reports of how Mrs Treble had met her death competed with firsthand accounts of close calls, narrow escapes and near misses. Mitchell was variously described as tall and well-built, small and scrawny; he had an unkempt bramble of dark brown hair on his chin or he was clean shaven. According to some eyewitness statements, the gunman prowled around town with an icy, deliberate cunning; others remembered the sailor being frantic and out-of-control. Yet others considered him scarcely human in appearance at all, a beast or a monster from the woods. He had the fierce, unblinking stare of a raptor and the wild gaze of a lunatic.

Right from the start the press portrayed the Petersfield shootings as the actions of a deranged sailor running amok through the streets, terrorising the populace, and firing indiscriminately and without warning at anyone who crossed his path ('shooting at all and sundry' is how the *Portsmouth Evening News* described it). The town had been spared a massacre only because the gunman's aim was so poor. Mrs Treble had been cold-bloodedly shot dead in the street — executed even — in front of her infant daughter, and the shooter had calmly walked away without showing any concern or remorse. This 'rampage' explanation quickly became the dominant narrative. Not once during the entire police investigation

39 'Awful Tragedy at Petersfield', *Hants and Sussex News*, 22 August 1906.

(such as it was) and the progress of the case through the criminal justice system did the authorities ever waver from this 'official' mainstream view.

The *Hampshire Post* naturally covered the story in considerable detail, but they weren't interested in raking over the details of the case to discover the truth of what had happened. They were content simply to report the pronouncements emanating from the coroner's court and the magistrates' office.

We need to go back and examine in detail what happened that afternoon in Station Road. We need to understand if the death of Mrs Treble was indeed the result of wilful murder, or an act of manslaughter, or perhaps even a terrible misadventure. And crucially, we need to determine who fired the fatal shot.

*

First, we must debunk the suggestion that Mitchell was firing indiscriminately at people in the street, and that his actions are an example of what in recent years has come to be known as 'rampage violence'.[40]

The testimony of Henry Birch, the chief firearms instructor at Tipner, indicates that Mitchell was a competent rifleman, maybe not a first-class shot but well able to hit a fixed target at a range of over 500 yards. Moreover, he was capable of quick, accurate shooting at short range (that is, snap shooting), and he demonstrated nerve and calmness in the field. Mitchell therefore had the means and the skill (and possibly the temperament) to shoot dead many people on that Friday afternoon had he so wished. But there is no evidence to suggest he was aiming to injure or maim anyone, let alone commit multiple homicides, and there is plenty of incontrovertible evidence to the contrary.

We have seen how he always discharged his bullets into bales of hay, or fired deliberately over the heads of his pursuers; we have noted how he aimed specifically for a bicycle wheel rather than at the cyclist. He shot into hedgerows and across open fields. Even when Goldsmith tried to run him over with his horse, and a soldier attempted to rob him of his gun and ammunition, he refrained from retaliating, opting instead to fire warning shots into the air. Admittedly, on many occasions he was reckless and showed wanton disregard for the safety of the public – it was only good fortune that saved Mrs Blackman and Mrs Steel from being hit by a bullet. When he fired over Dr Cross's back garden in Dragon Street, the bullet whizzed through the windows of the nearby Council offices, narrowly missing two men conversing in the forecourt. Undoubtedly, he was a serious menace. But he wasn't an aspiring rampage killer looking to pick off pedestrians one by one in the street. We have to ask how likely is it that Mitchell, who had been purposely aiming not to shoot anyone all day, should suddenly change modus operandi and fire directly at Mrs Treble and her child in Station Road, and then afterwards revert to purposely 'missing' again for the rest of the day until he was captured. And why would a gunman, intent on homicide, aim at the thigh?

40 A rampage is defined as the (attempted) killing of multiple persons in a public location in a single event by a lone actor, with victims chosen at random.

The testimony of William Aldridge

Let's look first at the testimony of William Herbert Aldridge. At around a quarter to five, as he was cycling over the level crossing heading into town, he heard the crack of a rifle. It wasn't so much the sound of gunfire that distracted him as the commotion at the corner of Charles Street, where a woman had fallen against the wall of the Railway Hotel stables. Aldridge lost control of his machine, he wobbled and fell off, tearing his left trouser knee as he struck the ground and grazing the skin of his leg.

William Aldridge was in his late thirties. He worked as a political agent for the Liberal Party in East Hampshire, undertaking secretarial and fundraising activities. He tended to move around from constituency to constituency: previously he had been based in Alton, but since 1906 he had resided at 5 Sandringham Road in Petersfield with his wife. Aldridge was a fussy little man, a bit of an ideologue, and a crushing bore. He was a keen draughts player, happy to sit by himself in front of a board for hours on end, analysing a position without touching any of the pieces. He might have pursued a political career of his own had it not been for his lack of charisma and a dithering inability to make decisions and stick to them that often manifested itself as spinelessness.

In 1893, while staying at Bournemouth, Aldridge had witnessed a fatality that so distressed him it appears to have induced some sort of mental breakdown. On 30 August he and an acquaintance called Harry Hussey went for an early morning bathe on the seafront at Boscombe. Despite the stormy weather, the strong easterly winds and a dangerously rough sea, the two men waded out into the water. Neither of them had noticed the lifebelt hanging on a post nearby. It wasn't long before Hussey got into trouble: he cramped up and felt himself being dragged out to sea. He screamed for help, but Aldridge was no use; desperate to save himself, he floundered back to shore, collapsing onto the beach in a state of fatigue. He had abandoned his companion, leaving him to drown. Another bather, William Richards, bravely swam out to Hussey, attempting a rescue, although by then it was too late. Aldridge's shame was compounded at the inquest the following day when the coroner pointedly ignored Aldridge, and commended Richards alone for 'doing his duty and acting a manly part'.[41]

Badly shaken, it seems Aldridge spent a few weeks recuperating at a nursing home somewhere inland, out of earshot of the waves breaking on the shore. He found comfort of sorts sitting on the veranda, playing board games in the weak autumn sunshine. Gradually he regained his wellbeing, and took his place once more in society, eventually finding work as a factotum at the Liberal and Radical Club in Tottenham. But he could never fully rid himself of guilt and a crippling sense that he had failed to act when tested.

Perhaps these thoughts were at the forefront of his mind when he heard gunshot and saw Margaret Treble collapse against the stable wall. Here, maybe,

41 'Sad drowning accident at Boscombe', *Brighton Guardian*, 2 September 1893.

was an opportunity for him to show spirit and pluck. Here, surely, he could do his duty and act a manly part. He wheeled his bicycle towards Mrs Treble, but then he spotted Mitchell coming up Station Road with a rifle in his arms. His nerve deserted him. Fortunately, the gates of Mr Richardson's dairy yard were open, so Aldridge dashed in there and hid in terror among the churns and wagons loaded with empty milk bottles. It was only after he had seen Mitchell stride past that he ventured out of the dairy and crossed the road to assist the injured woman, who by this time had been carried into the stable yard.

A small crowd had gathered round her. Someone noticed Aldridge with his torn trousers and bloodied knee entering the yard. It was then that Aldridge told his first big lie. Perhaps he was just caught up in the drama of the moment and blurted out an untruth unthinkingly, but his deception would have devastating consequences for himself and for Mitchell. Asked about his torn trouser leg, Aldridge claimed that he, too, had been shot by the sailor. The effect was immediate. Instantly he became one of the walking wounded (although the term was not in currency in 1906); he was a survivor of a mad gunman's rampage, bravely disregarding his own wounds to tend a fellow victim. Briefly, the shame of Boscombe beach was forgotten. He was a hero, although in truth all he had done is fall off his bicycle and cower among the milk bottles. And once the lie was told, it could not be taken back. He found himself expanding on the lie, fabricating further details to support the first falsehood. The bullet had rebounded off the stable wall, he said, and struck him as he was cycling past. The bullet knocked him off his bike. Yes, he saw Mitchell standing in the road, taking aim. He was only yards away from the gunman when he opened fire.

It was a disgraceful sham, and Aldridge will no doubt have regretted his actions even more when he was later called to give evidence at the inquest into Mrs Treble's death and then summoned as chief prosecution witness at Mitchell's committal hearing and subsequent trial. A lie on the spur of the moment, or rather a series of lies, made purely for vainglorious motives, would lead to perjury in the witness box at the crown court.

He gave his evidence three times — once at the inquest and twice in a court of law — and on each occasion he wore the same trousers he had been wearing on the day of the shooting. They became a kind of costume he donned when he went into the witness box to tell lies. The trouser leg hadn't been repaired — presumably, he wanted to show off this 'battle scar' as some sort of tangible proof of his testimony, but all it did was make him look like a tramp with a single pair of soiled trousers.

His evidence was a blatant pack of lies from start to finish, yet it was only during the inquest hearing that Aldridge's testimony came under any real scrutiny. First, the coroner wanted to know if Mitchell was standing or kneeling when he took aim — Aldridge said he was standing. Second, in the opinion of the witness, did Mitchell deliberately aim at the lady who dropped? Aldridge hesitated, conscious he was under oath and that to pin the blame for murder on

Mitchell would be a terrible injustice. He gave a typically vague and dithering response, suggesting that Mitchell may actually have fired at Fleet Goldsmith, who was standing between twelve and twenty yards further away down Charles Street on the opposite side of the road to Mrs Treble. This was a ludicrous suggestion. According to Aldridge, Mitchell fired at Fleet Goldsmith, the bullet glanced off him at right angles, travelled twenty yards, struck Mrs Treble in the thigh, penetrated the limb and deflected a second time at right angles off the stable wall, travelled a further half dozen yards across the road, and hit Aldridge in the leg as he was cycling into town. Thus, one bullet had supposedly hit three people. But Fleet Goldsmith hadn't been hit at all, and the impact site of Aldridge's minor injury was on the outside of his left leg. It would have been physically impossible for a bullet to strike the outside of Aldridge's left leg as he cycled eastwards down Station Road if the projectile had rebounded off the stable wall on the opposite side of the road.

Any competent coroner would have picked Aldridge up on all these contradictions, but instead Mr Edgar Goble merely pressed the witness on one point:

> Coroner: Can you tell us whether he took deliberate aim at the lady, or whether he fired quickly, and went away?
> Aldridge: To all intents and purposes, yes.
> Coroner: He took aim?
> Aldridge: Yes.

In this way, via a leading question from the coroner, Aldridge was urged to swear under oath that Mitchell had deliberately fired at Mrs Treble.

He finished off his evidence by stating that at the time of the murder Mitchell was wearing a Glengarry cap. The Glengarry cap is a woollen bonnet with a feather and rosette of ribbons worn by pipers in the Highlands of Scotland – ordinary ratings of the marine engineering class such as Mitchell wore a flat cap. Besides, as we know, Mitchell's cap (not even a Glengarry) had been stolen by Woolmer dragoons when he was drinking with them near Horndean earlier that day.

The testimony of Amelia Treble

Margaret Treble's sister-in-law, Amelia Maud, also gave evidence at the inquest, although she had little to say that touched on the actual murder. She confirmed simply that she had visited Petersfield that afternoon with Margaret, and on returning to the Railway Hotel stables her sister-in-law had been shot in the thigh. Margaret stood nearest the stable wall with Amelia on her right and the little child Doris trotting along between them. She couldn't say where the bullet came from and nor did she see anyone with a rifle. She only heard one shot being fired. She ran into the stable yard and fetched her brother; Margaret was then half-carried and half-dragged into the stable.

The testimony of Ralph Treble

Ralph Treble corroborated his sister's testimony. He had been in the stable yard talking to Albert Clarke when he heard the report of a rifle. Amelia came running up to him with the news that Margaret had been shot. He dashed outside. Believing Margaret had simply fainted he sent for some brandy, but when he was warned that an armed sailor was approaching up Station Road he helped carry Margaret into the stable yard for safety. He only heard the one shot.

The testimony of Douglas Fleet Goldsmith

For some reason Goldsmith didn't give evidence at the inquest hearing on Saturday afternoon. Perhaps he was too busy operating guided tours of the murder site. And nor did he present himself when the inquest resumed on Tuesday morning. The town had to wait for the committal hearing on Friday before they heard his account. In the end he provided a rather watered-down version of events, sensibly leaving out a lot of the made-up derring-do stuff about dodging bullets on horseback like Buffalo Bill; however, he still twisted the remaining facts to bolster his new-found celebrity as an all-action adventure hero. He claimed Mitchell opened fire on him at the top end of Charles Street, dropping on one knee and shooting directly at him. He had to jump to one side to avoid the bullet. He withdrew down Charles Street out of the line of fire.

According to Goldsmith, Mitchell fired twice in quick succession, the first bullet aimed at him and the second supposedly aimed at Mrs Treble. However, both Amelia Treble and Ralph Treble heard only the one gunshot, and even William Aldridge claimed just a single bullet had been fired. By his own account, Goldsmith admitted he did not actually witness the shooting of Mrs Treble at all. From where he was standing on Charles Street, he 'could not see either the deceased or the entrance to the stable'. He claimed he *heard* a second shot, which he assumed must have been Mitchell firing at Mrs Treble, although three other witnesses failed to hear this second shot. Therefore, the most likely interpretation is that Goldsmith invented the whole thing — he was neither shot at by Mitchell and nor did he witness Mitchell shooting at Mrs Treble.

The testimony of Albert Clarke

A fifth witness was Albert Clarke. The county coroner may have remembered the name because in August 1880 he held an inquest into the death of William Mellersh, a lad of fourteen, who had been fatally stabbed by a playmate in a country lane close to his home in Steep, near Petersfield. The accused boy was 10-year-old Albert Clarke. The two boys had a disagreement, leading to William punching Albert in the eye. Albert pulled out an ordinary penknife and during a struggle stabbed William in the lower chest with a backward swipe of the blade. A post-mortem revealed that the knife had penetrated the liver and heart, resulting in death from haemorrhage. The inquest jury announced a verdict of manslaughter, and Albert was committed for trial.[42]

The boy was considered 'intellectually backward' and he didn't seem to appreciate the seriousness of the proceedings: he frequently laughed during the inquest. Albert's father, William, was the licensee of the Harrow pub in Steep, which is where the inquest was held; the fact that the inquest took place effectively in the front room of Albert's house may have contributed to his sense of levity. His father was able to afford a good barrister,[43] and consequently the boy was acquitted at the Winchester Assizes in November 1880 on a plea that he acted in self-defence and was generally an inoffensive and well-behaved child.[44]

After the trial it seems there was considerable ill-feeling toward the Clarke family. The villagers stopped going to the Harrow pub, and William and Albert may have been hounded out of town. Albert became a coachman in Kennington, but returned to Steep around 1904. Two years later he found employment as a jobmaster at the Railway Hotel stables, and was on duty the afternoon Margaret Treble suffered her injuries.

Clarke proved to be a weak witness. His testimony came across as confused and conniving. He said he was talking with Mr Treble in the stable yard when he heard the sound of gunfire outside. Going out into the street, he saw Mitchell about twenty yards away on the other side of the road, hunkering down on one knee with his rifle raised. He just had time to notice Mrs Treble lying collapsed against the stable wall before Mitchell opened fire a second time, aiming directly at him. Clarke nimbly dodged back into the yard to avoid the bullet.

At the start of the inquest the coroner had quite properly told the jury that it was their job to find out how Mrs Treble had met her death, not to concern themselves over questions of whether or not the man who had done the act was sane or insane. Yet he couldn't resist questioning Clarke about Mitchell's appearance and demeanour. 'Did he look sane or like a maniac?' asked Goble. 'He looked like a man drilling,' replied Clarke. 'He advanced carrying the rifle and appeared to be quite calm. He did not say anything or shout out.'

Interestingly, Clarke's account resembles Goldsmith's version of events in so far as both men claimed *two* shots had been fired. This suggests they may have colluded to get their stories straight. But if they did, their scheming went horribly wrong. Clarke told the inquest jury that Mitchell's *first* bullet had felled Mrs Treble and that he [Clarke] was the intended target of the second; in contrast, Goldsmith testified at the magistrates' court that Mrs Treble had been felled by Mitchell's *second* bullet and that he [Goldsmith] was the intended target of the first.

42 'The fatal stabbing by a lad at Steep', *Hampshire Telegraph*, 11 August 1880.
43 He was Charles Mathews, the same barrister who eight years later would successfully defend eleven-year-old Robert Husband at his trial for the murder of Percy Searle. See David Green, *The Havant Boy Ripper* (Mango Books, 2018).
44 'A boys' quarrel and its result', *Hampshire Independent*, 17 November 1880.

Clarke never actually saw who shot Mrs Treble. He was inside the stable when he heard the fatal discharge. He assumed it was Mitchell who had fired, but that's all it was — an assumption.

And there are other inconsistencies with his evidence. Clarke claimed that Mitchell was kneeling in the road ready to take pot-shots at anyone who moved. Yet no one shot Amelia Treble when she rushed into the stables to fetch her brother, and no one shot Ralph Treble when he dashed out to be by Margaret's side. Mr Treble sent someone round to the Railway Hotel for a glass of brandy, but they weren't targeted either. In fact, Clarke went on to say that he himself ran out into the street to gather up some children and usher them to safety, but no one fired at Clarke or the children.

The truth is that Mitchell was halfway down Station Road when Margaret Treble was shot, at least 30-40 yards away. That is why Amelia Treble didn't see anyone when she looked round. This is substantiated by the testimony of Ralph Treble: when he and Amelia were leaning over Margaret by the stable wall, someone alerted them that an armed sailor was approaching up the street from the Catholic church. They quickly carried Mrs Treble into the stables, and a minute or two later Mitchell arrived at Mr Herridge's corner shop and asked directions from the proprietor.

The testimony of James Herridge

James Herridge wasn't called to give evidence at either the inquest or the committal hearing, but a journalist from the *Hampshire Chronicle* interviewed him about what he had seen that afternoon. Herridge's eyewitness account is important because it flatly contradicts the testimony of Aldridge, Goldsmith and Clarke, all of whom claimed they saw Mitchell standing (or kneeling) opposite Mr Herridge's shop at around the time Mrs Treble was shot. James Herridge was a hard-working and well-liked member of the community: he was secretary of the newly-built Methodist church in Station Road, and gave up a lot of his free time to act as piano accompanist at social gatherings in the town. When, in 1913, he decided to leave Petersfield to start a new life in Australia, his local Oddfellows lodge held a farewell smoking concert in his honour, presenting him with a gold signet ring as a token of their appreciation.[45]

He may have heard the crack of a rifle, or some other disturbance outside (perhaps Goldsmith hollering to Charles Hill to get out of the way, or the howl of a dog fleeing the scene), for he tells us he went outside and stood in his shop doorway, which faced onto Station Road. He didn't at this point apprehend that anyone had been shot; he didn't notice Mrs Treble slumped against the stable wall and he certainly didn't observe a gunman standing or kneeling in the road opposite his shop as stated by Aldridge, Goldsmith and Clarke. Shortly, he spotted Mitchell coming up the road from the direction of the Catholic church. As he approached the junction with Charles Street, he fired his rifle. Herridge thought

45 'Oddfellows' presentations to Mr J. H. Herridge', *Hants and Sussex News*, 25 June 1913.

nothing of it, believing the sailor was on manoeuvres and had aimed at military scouts on the other side of the level crossing. Mitchell stopped briefly outside the shop to ask directions. Herridge was not an unobservant man: he was used to dealing with the public, and a good judge of character; when he tells us that Mitchell behaved in a 'perfectly cool manner', we have to accept that this was how Mitchell presented himself. He evinced no concern over the injury to Mrs Treble because (like Herridge) he didn't know a woman had been shot, and by the time he passed the stable wall Margaret Treble had been carried into the yard.

The testimony of William Unsworth

The notable Arts and Crafts architect William Frederick Unsworth (1851-1912) had his offices in Petersfield, at the crossroads where Chapel Street and Tilmore Road meet Station Road.[46] No doubt he was interrupted by the commotion going on outside as Mitchell came along Chapel Street and turned left into Station Road, followed at a distance by a large crowd. He went outside to see what was going on, and according to the *Hampshire Chronicle* 'he saw [Mrs Treble] fall and ran across the road to her assistance'. He may well have done, although the murder site was not actually 'across the road' from Unsworth's office — it is over 100 yards away. However, even if true, there is no indication that Unsworth saw who fired the fatal shot.

The testimony of Charles May Mountford

Not much is known about Charles Mountford, and his eyewitness account (as reported in the *Hampshire Chronicle*) is equally vague and insubstantial. He was a single man in his mid-forties, originally from the New Alresford area; he appears to have come to Petersfield around the turn of the century to take up a position as acting manager of the Borough Brewery situated close to the railway at the south end of Frenchman's Road.[47]

He was cycling along Charles Street and had just turned right at Herridge's shop when he spotted Mitchell crossing the road near the Catholic church. The *Hampshire Chronicle* informs us that Mitchell fired the fatal shot as Mountford came round the corner, although Mountford never said that. He only saw an armed sailor standing further down the road with his rifle raised. Mountford was cycling towards Mitchell when the shot was fired, and of all the witnesses he had the best view of the alleged perpetrator at that critical moment. If he had seen Mitchell firing at Mrs Treble he would certainly have been called as a witness at the inquest and the committal hearing. Instead, his evidence strongly refutes

46 At the time it was numbered 16 Station Road.

47 The Borough Brewery, one of the last of Petersfield's breweries, was sold to Whitbread & Co in the early 1950s. The site is now occupied by the Amey Industrial Estate. See Nicholas Redman, 'The Breweries of Petersfield', *Bulletin Petersfield Area Historical Society*, Vol. 4, No. 8 (Autumn 1994), pp.8–12.

the testimony of Goldsmith, Aldridge and Clarke that Mitchell was standing (or kneeling) opposite Herridge's shop at the time of the shooting.

Mountford continued riding towards Mitchell. The *Chronicle* picks up the story:

> Before reaching the sailor he dismounted and wheeled his machine, keeping his eye on the man, and just before getting up to him the sailor nodded his head and remarked, 'You can pass', an injunction which needless to say, Mr Mountford promptly acted upon.[48]

According to Albert Clarke, Mitchell was kneeling in the road opposite Herridge's shop, ready to take pot-shots at anyone who moved, but Mountford's account flatly contradicts this. Mitchell was at least 30–40 yards further down the road when the shot was fired and he allowed Mountford to pass unmolested.[49]

*

By any standards, we can dismiss all the conflicting eyewitness accounts that have Mitchell kneeling or standing in the road opposite Herridge's corner shop, firing once or firing twice, aiming at different people, taking pot-shots, and wearing a Scottish piper's bonnet. They are simply fabrications from three witnesses who, for their own motives, sought to make capital out of the tragedy.

The evidence suggests the following sequence of events: Mitchell turns left up Station Road, passes the Catholic church, and starts to cross the road diagonally to reach Herridge's corner shop. A shot is heard. Mrs Treble collapses against the stable wall. Aldridge falls off his bicycle. Goldsmith spots Mitchell coming up Station Road and retreats down Charles Street. Charles Hill dashes for cover. Mountford passes Mitchell. Margaret Treble is carried into the stables. Mitchell fires over the level crossing. Mitchell asks directions from James Herridge. Mitchell passes the Railway stables and crosses the railway line.

At the inquest, the coroner concluded, 'It was impossible a case of murder could be more clearly, more distinctly brought home . . . There was no other course open [to the jury] in the present case than to return a verdict of wilful murder.' But in this book I am arguing that there is every reason to believe that Margaret Treble was *not* shot by Mitchell. There is no doubt whatsoever that Mrs Treble was struck by a bullet and that she subsequently died of her wounds, and there is no dispute that Mitchell was armed and firing his rifle as he walked up Station Road. But there is no evidence that Mitchell fired the fatal shot. In the next chapter we will consider the serious deficiencies in the coroner's enquiry that led to Mitchell being wrongly indicted for wilful murder. For now, though, we need to ask the vital question: if Mitchell didn't shoot Margaret Treble, who did?

48 *Hampshire Chronicle*, 25 August 1906.
49 The *Hampshire Advertiser*, in their coverage of the 'sensational shooting in Hampshire' misidentified this witness as 'a farmer called Warren'. See 'A Sailor's Frenzy', *Hampshire Advertiser*, 25 August 1906.

*

We have seen how Mitchell entered Petersfield via The Causeway, crossing the Forebridge and making his way up Dragon Street and through the town centre to the railway station. There were extraordinary scenes as members of the public scattered before him. A large crowd gathered in his wake, trailing the gunman. Often, Mitchell would turn round and level his weapon at the mob, causing them to flee or scurry for cover. The police were unarmed,[50] and totally unable to get near their man to effect a capture. In his evidence at the inquest, Police Sergeant Joseph Allen explained the difficult they faced:

> Coroner: You could not get at him?
> PS Allen: No, it was impossible. He was holding the rifle like this [indicating the position], and for the very first person who attempted to go up to him it would have been certain death to him. It would have been madness to have gone towards him.

Mitchell marched quickly through the town, sometimes breaking into a run, at other times pausing to consider his route; his pursuers generally kept at what they thought was a safe distance. Yet there were others, like Douglas Fleet Goldsmith, who took a more direct approach, obtaining firearms of their own and actively coursing the sailor. The bloodlust of the hue and cry was never far away. Farmers and poachers hurried home to fetch their loaded shotguns from stable or cellar; army veterans brought out their old muskets.

Take William Goble, for instance, the licensee of the Railway Hotel.[51] Like all decent, law-abiding pub landlords, he had a crate of unexploded hand grenades in an upstairs room at the hotel. Hearing that a crazed stranger with a service rifle was going berserk in Station Road, he ran out into the street with a grenade, intending to hurl it at the gunman. Fortunately for everyone, Mitchell had already crossed the railway line and was heading out to Rushes Farm; one of the police constables trailing Mitchell had quiet words with Goble and persuaded him to put the grenade down and return to his customers.

There was also William J. Tew, grocer, wine and spirits merchant, dairyman and shop keeper of 20 Lavant Street. Let's look at William Tew for a moment.

*

William John Tew was born in Steep in 1867. He grew up on Sole Farm on the edge of the Weald.[52] His father died in 1891 and the family home was sold a few years later, but William had already moved out by then. He married Sarah Berry

50 Apparently, until the early 1980s the Petersfield police only had access to a single revolver kept in a safe in the Chief Inspector's office. See Steve Sargent, 'A Short History of Petersfield Police Station', *Bulletin Petersfield Area Historical Society*, Vol. 7, No. 1 (Spring 2006), p.5.
51 No relation to Edgar Goble, the coroner.
52 Bedales School is a five minute walk away across the fields.

in Portsmouth in 1889 and the following year bought a house in Station Road in Petersfield, where he worked as a dairyman.

Tew was very much a self-made man, full of indomitable energy and motivated by grand schemes. In 1892 he purchased premises at 20 Lavant Street and opened his Alderney Dairy, selling cream, fresh butter, new laid eggs and poultry and pure new milk. Always diversifying, he soon became the agent for Lipton's Tea and by 1895 had added confectionery, groceries, tobacco products and all kinds of temperance drinks to his stock. In 1899 he was granted an excise licence to sell wine, liquors and spirits.

He threw himself into various civic and leisure activities, becoming honorary secretary of the Petersfield St John's Ambulance Association and a member of the Petersfield Chess Club.[53] The town was excited to get its first horse-drawn fire engine in 1889: a volunteer fire brigade, comprising fourteen men, was formed shortly afterwards, and Tew was involved right from the start, serving twelve years as secretary and six as captain. He felt at home riding on the Brigade's new Shand Mason steam fire engine purchased in 1904, racing round the town and surrounding villages squirting jets of water 120 feet into the air.

Around 1896 he joined the 3rd (Volunteer) Battalion of the Hampshire Regiment. The Hampshires were an infantry regiment created as part of the Childers Reforms in 1881. The Volunteer movement was well organised and supported in Hampshire, and they became pioneers in military cycling. Tew actually joined a bicycle battalion: kitted out in knickerbockers, black stockings and box-cloth spats, he and his fellow recruits went on stealth manoeuvres around the Petersfield countryside, carrying their binoculars and service revolvers in haversacks. They were trained to act as scouts and messengers (and later as stretcher bearers). Tew rose to the rank of captain.

By 1901 Tew had diversified again, capitalising on his military experiences and going into business as a bicycle engineer, dealer and repairer. He opened a cycle shop on Charles Street.

*

Over the years Tew took part in many musketry competitions and shooting tournaments. He seemed to enjoy the social side of these events more than the competitive element, in the same way he welcomed the friendship at his local chess club but lost most of his games. Occasionally he won a small cash prize for finishing in one of the lower placings at a rifle tourney, but he was not by any means a proficient shot.

A report in the *Hampshire Chronicle* tells us that Captain Tew was among the mob tailing Mitchell up Station Road. Senior police officers such as Superintendent King and Sergeant Allen had broken off from the main group to head up Lavant Street. As chief of the Fire Brigade, Tew may have stepped in to assume de facto command of the main pursuing party; the crowd will have

53 Charles Mountford and Charles Hill were also members of the chess club.

deferred to him, allowing him to move to the front line of the posse. Being the only armed individual among them, he will have been their best hope of taking out Mitchell before he seriously injured anyone. Tew crept closer to his man.

When Mitchell passed the Catholic church he crossed the road diagonally, heading for Herridge's corner shop. Tew must have calculated that this gave him the clearest sighting of his target and the best chance of taking him down. He raised his gun and fired at Mitchell.

Captain Tew ought to have known better. It was extremely reckless to open fire in the street like that. Tew's military training and his experience in shooting competition had only prepared him for firing at fixed targets at known distances; he had no skill for judging distance or for aiming at moving and fleeting targets. Nor was he accustomed to the added risk of shooting at a target that might well turn around and return the fire. All these factors must have considerably disadvantaged his aim.

The *Hampshire Chronicle* admitted that 'Mr Tew had fired at the fugitive but without effect'. A blunter way of saying the same thing is to state quite simply that Tew missed. Worse still, he was so focused on Mitchell, he did not notice the Trebles moving into the line of fire further up the road by the stable walls. The bullet whizzed past Mitchell and struck Mrs Treble in the thigh.

Did Tew realise he had hit an innocent member of the public? Possibly. He must have seen Mrs Treble collapse against the stable wall, just as William Unsworth had.

Tew carried on pursuing Mitchell up the Winchester Road. As he passed the Railway Hotel stables and made his way across the railway line, it seems the fire chief gave no thought to Margaret Treble. Tew was a member of the St John's Ambulance Brigade and trained in first aid and emergency life-saving techniques: it is a pity he never considered intervening to help Mrs Treble, who even then was bleeding to death in the stable yard from the bullet fired from his gun.

4

'Downright murder'

When Dr Robert Cross arrived at the Railway Hotel stables, he found Margaret Treble lying on the ground 'in a complete state of collapse'. She had gone into shock from loss of blood. Looking under her skirts he quickly found the cause — a nasty, jagged wound about one and a half inches in length in the anterior upper third of her right thigh. She was still bleeding profusely. He sent Ralph Treble to fetch a tourniquet from Dr Panckridge's surgery at Winton House; meanwhile he did his best to arrest the flow of blood by applying pressure to the wound.

By the time Ralph returned, Margaret had been placed on a stretcher (secured from the railway Station) and was being transported to the Cottage Hospital near The Spain. Dr Cross advised Mr Treble that the best course of action was for him to take Amelia and the little girl back to Peake Farm.

At the hospital, Dr Cross examined the injury in closer detail. The bullet had missed the thigh bone but completely lacerated the femoral artery and vein, the main vessels that carry blood between the heart and the lower body. Deep inside the wound he found two pieces of metal, which he identified as fragments of a purse clasp. Dr Cross concluded that the bullet had passed through the purse in Mrs Treble's pocket before entering the thigh: the collision with the clasp and with two coins in the purse had flattened the head of the bullet, effectively converting the missile into a dumdum bullet that expanded on impact. In the doctor's opinion, this explanation sufficiently accounted for the terrible nature of the entry wound and the extensive haemorrhaging. In support of his theory, Dr Cross located a star-shaped hole in the purse corresponding to some degree with the entrance wound in the thigh.

Margaret was in a serious condition, and despite Dr Cross and the hospital staff doing everything they could, she deteriorated quickly and died about half-past six the same evening.

*

In Dr Cross's view, Mrs Treble's death was 'absolutely due to loss of blood caused by the bullet wound'. For this reason he told the coroner he felt there was no need to perform an autopsy. If there had been any doubt as to the cause of death, or any need to collect evidence to support a criminal prosecution, then the coroner will have ordered a post mortem. But at the time of the inquest the authorities were satisfied that Mrs Treble had died at the hands of Herbert Mitchell, hence no request for a post mortem was made.

In 1906 forensic ballistics was still in its infancy, but a considerable body of research existed in medical journals detailing the characteristic features of gunshot injuries inflicted by the Lee-Metford rifle at short and long range. Had a thorough post mortem been undertaken, forensic evidence will have been obtained that might well have determined which weapon — a Lee-Metford MKII or some other firearm — had fired the fatal shot.

Another way of determining which weapon had been used in the assault would have been to examine the make of bullet that had perforated Mrs Treble's limb. At the inquest the coroner asked Superintendent King if the bullet had been recovered, but the officer admitted they weren't able to find it. After exiting Mrs Treble's thigh, it had presumably rebounded off the stable wall into the road, where possibly a member of the posse tailing Mitchell, or one of the tourist ghouls, had pocketed it as a souvenir. Either way, it was very convenient for Captain Tew that the one piece of evidence that would have conclusively linked the bullet to his gun had 'gone missing'. Here was criminal justice at its finest in Petersfield: a medical practitioner uninterested in performing an autopsy on a murder victim; witnesses like James Aldridge, Fleet Goldsmith and Albert Clarke coming forward with their fabricated evidence to falsely accuse Herbert Mitchell; and now the tell-tale bullet mysteriously disappearing from the crime scene that was never properly secured by the police in the first place . . . all these developments worked considerably to Captain's Tew's advantage, leading him to hope that his actions on the day of Mrs Treble's death might avoid scrutiny altogether.

*

Robert Cross was a native of Petersfield. Educated at Marlborough College, he qualified as a physician in 1886 and went on to train as a house surgeon at St Bartholomew's in London. The following year he succeeded to his father's practice in Petersfield, taking up a junior partnership with Dr Charles Ticehurst. Cross rose quickly to become one of the town's most prominent citizens: he acted for many years as Medical Officer of Health for the Petersfield Rural District and the Union Workhouse, and for over a quarter of a century he served as secretary (later president) of the Petersfield Cottage Hospital, which his father had helped to found.

Dr Cross was also a Justice of the Peace and a founding member and three-times Chairman of the Urban District Council. His other activities included a stint as Governor of Churcher's College, Chairman of the Petersfield and District Building Society, and a director of the Petersfield Laundry Company. A prominent Freemason, he was a Past Master of the 'Lodge of Friendship' in Petersfield.[54]

At best he was a charming and kind man, greatly revered by his patients for his unfailingly gracious bedside manner and his assiduous medical care. But there was another side to him. He could be peevish if his judgment was questioned and stubborn if he didn't get his own way. The solicitous family doctor with the rich, resonant baritone voice was also the curmudgeonly magistrate who

54 For details of Dr Cross's life and career, see the obituaries in the *Hampshire Telegraph*, 11 November 1932, and the *West Sussex Gazette*, 10 November 1932. See also Bill Gosney, 'Four Doctors named Robert Cross', *Bulletin Petersfield Area Historical Society*, Vol.9, No. 2 (Autumn 2016), pp.9–12. Douglas Fleet Goldsmith was a member of the same lodge.

thought nothing of sentencing a beggar to seven days' hard labour for asking a grocer for some bread and cheese. The theft of a bicycle piqued his wrath and he handed down an intemperate three months' prison sentence. Like many small town dignitaries, he had an overweening sense of entitlement: he once badgered the Chief Constable of Hampshire to divert precious police resources into a sting operation aimed at catching a bricklayer from Liss Forest who was stealing eggs from a turkey nest in Dr Cross's garden.[55] When, in June 1903, Dr Cross himself appeared before the Petersfield Petty Sessions charged with dangerous driving near Langrish, he oozed indignation and wasted the court's time with special pleading, arguing that the law of the land did not apply to him.[56]

*

In the hectic hours following the shooting of Mrs Treble, Dr Cross was also called to the police station to examine Herbert Mitchell's wounds. Fleet Goldsmith had shot him twice — once in the back of the head, and a second time in the small of the back (or the back of the legs) — but both injuries turned out to be minor and of no great significance.

From the outset, everything about the police handling of the case deviated from usual procedure. Mitchell was arrested outside the Seven Stars in Stroud, but according to the arresting officer, Constable Charles Stockwell, the prisoner was never formally cautioned. He was taken to the police station in handcuffs, and locked in one of the three cells. They were dismal chambers with brick vaulted ceilings and stone floors, and 'mighty wooden doors bearing huge locks and bolts'.[57] The police eventually got round to interviewing their suspect on Saturday morning, yet even then (according to Stockwell) they failed to administer the obligatory caution before doing so. This failure to caution Mitchell at the time of arrest and prior to questioning means that the evidence secured by the police, even if voluntarily offered by Mitchell, was improperly obtained and technically inadmissible in court.

There was another concern. Around seven o'clock on Friday evening, Dr Cross took it upon himself to question Mitchell in his cell about the shooting spree. It isn't clear under what authority Dr Cross was permitted to interview the suspect. It was certainly highly irregular. Mitchell was not apprised of his right to remain silent, and he was not afforded the right to have legal representation at the station.

As it happens, Mitchell had little to say to Dr Cross about the death of Mrs Treble. He pretended to have no recollection at all of the day's adventure. He told the doctor the only incident he could vaguely recall was assisting a soldier with a damaged bicycle outside Petersfield. We will examine Mitchell's state of mind,

55 *Hants and Sussex News*, 3 May 1899.
56 *Hants and Sussex News*, 24 June 1903.
57 Steve Sargent, 'A Short History of Petersfield Police Station', *Bulletin Petersfield Area Historical Society*, Vol. 7, No. 1 (Spring 2006), p.3.

his conduct and his course of action in a later chapter. For now, we need simply to observe how easily Dr Cross was hoodwinked by Mitchell. He told the inquest jury:

> His mind appeared to have been a blank from the time he got on to the range at Tipner in the morning . . . I do not think he realised that he had been shot himself. He said his head was aching very much.

Dr Cross interviewed Mitchell a second time on Saturday morning, again not under caution. Mitchell repeated his story that he had no recollection of the previous day's events. But on this occasion he spoke to the doctor at length about his troubled career in the Navy and about his criminal past. These revelations, which were highly prejudicial, cemented the view of the authorities that the sailor was a dangerous, demented individual who had shot Margaret Treble in cold blood.

*

On Saturday 18 August, at eleven o'clock in the morning, Mitchell was brought before the magistrates at the Petty Sessional Court. A magistrates' and coroner's court had been built behind the police station in St Peter's Road in the 1890s,[58] so Mitchell didn't have far to travel. After breakfast in his cell, and the interrogation sessions with Cross and Sergeant Allen, he was marched across the courtyard and into court.

> He looked none the worse for his experience of the previous day, and appeared perfectly calm and collected, and in his right senses. He is a well-built, muscular young fellow, stated to be 22 years of age, but appeared somewhat older, with dark hair and complexion.[59]

On the bench sat Sydney Hylton Jolliffe, a former Member of Parliament for Petersfield, and Captain Percy Seward. The courtroom was packed: among the spectators at the back of the hall could be seen Lieutenant Steele of HMS *Nelson*.

Mitchell was formally charged with the wilful murder of Margaret Treble. As the charge was being read out, 'the prisoner's eyes were directed upon the floor, and his fingers twitched nervously as they hung by his sides'.[60] Only one witness, Sergeant Allen, gave evidence; he told the court that earlier that morning he had cautioned and then charged Mitchell with the killing of Mrs Treble. The prisoner had made no reply. Sergeant Allen made sure he recited to the court the actual words of the caution so that there could be no doubt in the minds of the

58 Diana Syms, 'The origins of Policing in Petersfield', *Bulletin Petersfield Area Historical Society*, Vol. 9, No. 4 (Autumn 2017), pp.3–7.
59 *Hampshire Chronicle*, 25 August 1906.
60 *Hampshire Post*, 24 August 1906.

magistrates that the proper police procedure had been followed.[61] But Sergeant Allen was playing games: he knew full well that after his arrest Mitchell had been questioned by Cross, and of course by himself, for several hours without being cautioned.

Asked by the Deputy Justices' Clerk if he wished to put any questions to the Sergeant, Mitchell replied, 'No, sir. Thank you.' Superintendent King then applied for a remand till Friday to enable the police to continue their inquiries.

The proceedings had lasted no more than ten minutes. The prisoner was taken back to the cells. Mitchell indicated to Superintendent King that he did not wish to attend the inquest scheduled for later that afternoon, so after lunch, accompanied by two police officers, he was escorted to the railway station and put on the 1.19 train to Portsmouth. A cab took him the rest of the way to Kingston prison.

*

Mitchell's master plan to feign partial or total amnesia quickly came unstuck. By claiming he couldn't remember the events of Friday 17 August, he effectively put himself in a position where he was unable to refute the false accusations made against him. Perhaps this is one reason why he declined to attend the inquest.

At 4.15 on Saturday afternoon the coroner for South Hampshire, Edgar Goble of Fareham, opened the inquiry into Margaret Treble's death. Goble was nearly in his seventies, and coming to the end of his long career. During his service as coroner, Goble had conducted many important Admiralty cases such as the disaster of the ill-fated Royal Navy submarine *A1*, which sank in the Solent in 1904 with the loss of all hands.[62] Goble's father had been on board the HMS *Victory* at Trafalgar and he had dined with Nelson on the eve of the battle.

A twelve-man jury was sworn in, with the newspaper proprietor A. W. Childs chosen as foreman. Among the jurors was Edward Fenn, who had driven the van conveying Mitchell from Stroud to the police station.

The first duty of the jurors was to follow Mr Goble over to the Cottage Hospital mortuary to view the body of the deceased. Back at the court house, they heard evidence relating to identification and cause of death. Ralph Treble, after identifying the body as that of his sister-in-law, Margaret, recounted the events of Friday afternoon as best he could remember them.

The second witness was Dr Cross. He deposed to being sent for just after 4.30 on Friday.[63] He described finding Mrs Treble in a state of collapse from loss of blood. She was taken to the Cottage Hospital where she died in his presence at approximately six-thirty. There was no doubt in the doctor's mind that death

61 'I am about to charge you with a serious offence, but before I do so I caution you that whatever you may say I shall take down in writing, and it will be used in evidence against you or for you.'
62 Goble also presided at the inquest into the death of Percy Searle, an eight-year-old schoolboy murdered in Havant in 1888. See David Green, *The Havant Boy Ripper* (Mango Books, 2018).
63 Mrs Treble was shot at around a quarter to five, so the doctor will have been summoned closer to 4.50.

was due to loss of blood caused by the bullet wound. He explained to the jury his theory about how the bullet had picked up metal fragments from Mrs Treble's purse clasp before entering the body, thereby imparting a more serious injury to the victim: 'The probability was if this bullet had entered her thigh without touching the purse her life might have been saved.'

After expressing the court's sympathy to the family of the deceased, the coroner adjourned the inquest until Tuesday 21 August.

*

When the inquest resumed at eleven o'clock on Tuesday morning, the small court house was even more crowded than on Saturday. Once the jury and the police had taken their places, there was little room left for anyone else. The remaining seats were filled with reporters and relatives of the deceased, along with representatives of the Admiralty and several Naval and other witnesses. A considerable number of town people congregated in front of the police station, hoping to catch sight of the accused as he arrived for the hearing, but they were disappointed. Mitchell had again declined to attend.

Edgar Goble entered the courtroom accompanied by his clerk and a shorthand writer. After he had taken his seat, the adjourned inquest got under way.

Amelia Treble was the first witness. She described going into town with her sister-in-law on Friday. In a barely audible whisper, she related the terrible events outside the Railway Hotel stables. 'After she heard the shot my sister-in-law turned to me and said "I am shot", and fell down.'

William Aldridge and Albert Clarke were next up. We have already assessed their dubious testimony in Chapter 3. Aldridge actually limped into court, drawing attention to his torn trouser leg. Neither of them was able to formally identify the accused because Mitchell wasn't in court; however, both men stated they felt certain they would be able to identify the man if they saw him again, and that was good enough for the coroner. A rifle was then brought into court by the police. The coroner told Aldridge it was the same type of rifle that Mitchell had been carrying on the day in question. Astonishingly, he then asked the witness, 'Is this the kind of rifle he was carrying on the day in question?' 'Yes,' replied Aldridge. This was another of Aldridge's lies. He'd been hiding behind the milk bottles when Mitchell marched past — he could scarcely have caught a good look at the weapon, besides which he probably didn't know enough about firearms anyway to confidently distinguish the Lee-Metford from any other service rifle, although he did notice that the bayonet wasn't attached. The inquest seemed to be proceeding on the basis that the man in custody, Herbert Mitchell, was incontestably responsible for killing Mrs Treble: Mitchell's guilt was presented to the jury almost as a fait accompli, and any concerns the coroner ought to have had over suspect identification and the reliability and truthfulness of witness testimony never surfaced during the hearing.

Now it was the turn of the police. Constable Charles Stockwell of the Hampshire Constabulary, stationed at Petersfield, gave a vivid account of chasing Mitchell along the Winchester Road. At one point he took to mimicking the actions of the sailor, pointing a pretend rifle in the direction of the jury bench and moving the gun from one juror to the next — from Childs to Boyt to Duffett to Poulter to Fenn — like a rabbit hunter primed to shoot at anything that suddenly moved. Stockwell lived in Penns Road, just the other side of the level crossing; technically he was off duty when a tradesman alerted him to the commotion at the gate. He went out and spotted the gunman about a hundred yards away, near the Volunteer Arms. Stockwell joined the hue and cry. According to the policeman's evidence, Mitchell fired four or five times at his pursuers, although in truth the bullets sailed harmlessly above the crowd, landing in the fields. Like Goldsmith, he tried in vain to get in front of Mitchell by squeezing through a gap in the hedge and racing across the meadows. He estimated to being perhaps 30 yards behind Goldsmith when the auctioneer opened fire: the fugitive 'went down face forwards,' he said.

The coroner commented sourly on Goldsmith's absence from court. He seemed to believe Goldsmith ought to have made the effort to attend.

Mr Percy Burley,[64] appearing on behalf of the relatives of the deceased, asked the coroner if evidence would be brought before the inquiry as to Mitchell firing through the town. In the coroner's view, such evidence was not strictly relevant to the question of how the deceased came to her death, so he was inclined not to include it. Yet the next witness, Police Sergeant Joseph Allen, proceeded to recount to the court how he had seen Mitchell firing through the town. He claimed Mitchell shot at him, and at Constable Pullman, as they crossed the Forebridge, although that wasn't true — as we have seen, Mitchell discharged his weapon over the roofs of the town. Allen concluded his evidence by describing the capture of the prisoner and his treatment at the police station.

*

After an adjournment for lunch, Dr Cross was recalled. He spoke briskly about administering first aid to Mitchell in the police cells, making it sound as if the act of cleaning and dressing a small graze was somehow beneath him, almost an affront to his status as a senior medical practitioner.

One of the witnesses bound over to appear at the adjourned inquest was George Wilson, the medical officer attached to HMS *Nelson*. He was due to give evidence on Mitchell's mental history, but a 'sharp attack of inflammation' had caused him to take to his bed. Regrettably he could not attend the hearing. A graduate of the University of Edinburgh Medical School, he had entered the Navy as a surgeon in 1887. During his early career he saw action in Kenya and Zanzibar. He was promoted to Staff Surgeon in 1899 and Fleet Surgeon in 1903. With an eye

64 Mr Burley played the organ at the Wesleyan Methodist church on Station Road, just down from Herridge's corner shop.

on his looming early retirement (April 1907), Wilson was anxious to avoid any scandal that might tarnish his reputation: no doubt he was grateful for an excuse to distance himself from the Mitchell affair, which was quickly turning into a major embarrassment for the Admiralty.[65]

It fell, therefore, to Dr Cross to apprise the court of Mitchell's background and mental history. But whereas Wilson's overview would have been based to some extent on clinical records of previous illnesses and hospitalisations, all Cross had to go on was the prisoner's recounting of his own life. As we will see in the next chapter, Mitchell's self-reported biography is difficult to verify.

Another problem was that Cross had no training in the diagnosis of mental illness and no experience in the psychiatric evaluation of homicide defendants. He didn't know how to distinguish malingering and feigned mental illness from genuine personality disorders. His knowledge in these areas was almost non-existent. His conclusions on Mitchell's mental state were therefore inevitably dubious and of limited evidential value. The coroner ought to have recognised Dr Cross's limitations of competence and Cross himself should have been circumspect about testifying in a case for which he lacked the necessary expertise.[66]

Cross told the inquiry that Mitchell had no memory of being in Petersfield on Friday. His mind was apparently a blank from the time he left Tipner firing range on Friday morning until he found himself in the cells at the police station. This localized amnesia was not brought on by any physical trauma to the skull (the first bullet that struck Mitchell had merely grazed the back of the head), and nor could it be accounted for by the effects of alcohol or any other drug (although the prisoner has been drinking on the day in question). Rather, in the doctor's opinion, the loss of memory was characteristic of a fugue state associated with post-epileptic mania.[67] Post-epileptic mania emerged as a new psychiatric category in the late nineteenth century: in a lecture on epilepsy in 1902, the English neurologist William Broadbent drew attention to the 'maniacal excitement of extreme violence' that sometimes occurred after an epileptic seizure. 'Homicide,' he stated, 'has not infrequently been committed in paroxysms of epileptic mania.'[68] These states of post-epileptic mania were often associated

65 The *Hampshire Chronicle* was obliged to issue a clarification after they misrepresented his involvement in the case: 'We are requested to explain that Fleet Surgeon G Wilson is the Medical Officer attached to His Majesty's ship *Nelson*, that he is in no way connected with Haslar [the military hospital at Gosport], and had nothing to do with the discharge of Mitchell.' (*Hampshire Chronicle*, 25 August 1906.)
66 An example of Dr Cross's poor judgment, and an illustration of the way his testimony was often privileged to the detriment of commonsense, can be seen in the evidence he gave at the coroner's inquiry into the death of farmer Henry Luggar, who had committed suicide at Langrish in 1904 by blowing the top of his face and head off with a double-barrelled rabbit shooting gun. At the inquest Cross had risibly suggested that Luggar, an experienced sportsman, had been cleaning his loaded gun and was looking down the barrel when somehow the trigger was accidentally pulled. See 'Gun fatality at Langrish', *Hants & Sussex News*, 5 October 1904.
67 'Fugue' comes from the Latin word for 'flight'. The term refers not simply to an episode of confusion or lost memory but to a period of bewildered wandering or sudden and unplanned travel away from home.
68 William Broadbent, 'A Lecture on Epilepsy', *British Medical Journal* Vol. 1, No. 2140 (4 January 1902), p.1.

with complete amnesia for the events of the crime. Under questioning from Dr Cross, Mitchell described a seven-year history of fits and seizures accompanied by outbursts of violence and memory loss. He also admitted to the doctor that his father was at present in an asylum. Based on these 'facts', Cross felt emboldened to offer his opinion on Mitchell's soundness of mind to the court:

> From his previous history, and from his demeanour, I came to the conclusion that he was a man subject to these fits of what were called post-epileptic mania, and during these attacks he is in no way responsible for his actions.

The role of the expert witness was to assist the jury in determining facts outside their common understanding, yet Cross himself was a layman with no special knowledge of insanity or criminal law and only a fragmentary acquaintance with the details of Mitchell's case. While he may have conferred privately with medical men from Haslar hospital in Gosport before tendering his opinion on the state of Mitchell's mind, his lack of professional training and expertise ought to have disqualified him from pronouncing opinions and conclusions in court. After all, they were just the opinions and conclusions of a country doctor pontificating on subjects he knew nothing about. He ought to have restricted his evidence to giving facts and saying what he knew instead of usurping the function of the jury.

The inquest was turning into a farce. Witnesses were falsely accusing Mitchell of murder, Mitchell himself was feigning loss of memory for a crime he hadn't committed, and a general practitioner who knew nothing about madness was declaring the prisoner insane.

The inept double-act of coroner Goble and Dr Cross continued:

> Coroner: I think in these cases a man may go on for some years without showing anything whatever is the matter with him?
> Dr Cross: That is so.
> Coroner: And supposing a medical man is called in is it impossible to detect there is anything the matter with him except for his previous history?
> Dr Cross: Certainly his previous history is a guide to us.
> Coroner: We, of course, cannot go into the question of his insanity.

In the end, it took a series of direct question from Percy Burley to expose Cross's lack of credentials:

> Mr Burley: Is he [Mitchell] a man who should be allowed to be at large?
> Dr Cross: I think the medical man from Haslar would better answer the question than I could.
> Mr Burley: You would not like to express an opinion?
> Dr Cross: No.

*

The next witness was Henry Birch, first-class petty officer on board HMS *Nelson* and musketry instructor at Tipner. Birch testified to the amount of ammunition issued to Mitchell over the course of the week's firearms training. The main question that needed answering was how could Mitchell smuggle close to thirty rounds of ammunition out of the firing camp? Birch was anxious to save face and deflect criticism of compliance practices at Tipner; his testimony failed to provide any explanations at all, and by constantly touting the supposedly top-notch safety procedures at Tipner his evidence served only to further deepen the mystery of how so much ammunition went missing.

Warrant Officer Walter Rose gave details of Mitchell's disappearance and the half-hearted efforts to locate him. He told the court he had been in overall charge of the rifle range at Tipner for four years but this was the first time a man had broken away from the range with a rifle and ammunition. He thought Mitchell might have 'slunk away to have a drink' in one of the pubs in Stamshaw, so he didn't bother searching for him or reporting him missing till after lunch, by which time Mitchell was miles away in the Hampshire countryside.

Some startling and very disturbing testimony came next from William Windsor, sick bay steward on board HMS *Nelson*. Dr Cross had alluded to this evidence earlier, but now the full shocking story came out. It is worth reproducing part of the account from the inquest:

> Wm. Windsor: About 11 o'clock on the 19th July I was in the sick bay, and heard someone crying out "Help! Murder!" I went and found Harry Bentley, a second-class stoker, and Herbert Mitchell [Joseph Burbidge] struggling together.[69]
> Coroner: Did Mitchell have an open razor in one hand and a bottle of lotion in the other?
> Wm. Windsor: Yes, Sir.
> Coroner: And before you got to them did Bentley knock the bottle out of the hand of Mitchell?
> Wm. Windsor: Yes, out of his right hand, Sir.
> Coroner: And did he take hold of the razor with his other hand?
> Wm. Windsor: Yes.
> Coroner: Then did Mitchell seize Bentley by the throat?
> Wm. Windsor: Yes.
> Coroner: And took the razor out of his hand?
> Wm. Windsor: Mitchell seized Bentley by the throat, and I took the razor out of Mitchell's hand. It took several men to hold Mitchell down.

Mitchell was immediately placed under guard in his hammock. The incident was a curious one because there was no ill-feeling between the two men – they were actually very good friends, and Mitchell always seemed 'a jolly chap about the ship, dancing and singing'. It was almost as if the two shipmates were

69 Mitchell had joined the Royal Navy under the assumed name 'Joseph Burbidge'.

engaging in a mock brawl, putting on a fake fighting scene just at the moment when Windsor was close by and able to 'intervene'.

Harry Bentley, a second-class stoker on board HMS *Nelson* and the 'victim' of the assault, also gave evidence at the inquest. He described how he had just entered the sick bay when he came across Mitchell sitting there with a bottle of lotion in one hand and a razor in the other, apparently on the brink of committing suicide by cutting his own throat. Then, suddenly, for no reason all, Mitchell tried to force Bentley to swallow the lotion, which Bentley thought was poisonous. He grabbed hold of Mitchell's wrist but Mitchell poured the liquid over Bentley's shoulder, drenching his uniform. The stokers fell to the floor in a tussle. At that point, Windsor came to his assistance.

Next morning Mitchell was examined by Fleet-Surgeon George Wilson. Despite behaving like a madman the previous day, Mitchell now appeared placid and rational. He claimed to have no recollection whatsoever of the incident with the razor and the bottle of lotion. Nonetheless, Wilson ordered his removal under escort to Haslar hospital where he was put in a 'maniac's ward' for observation.

It seems Mitchell was only kept in a Haslar for a fortnight, because on 2 August he was 'discharged, cured'. When the sick bay steward was asked by Mr Burley why Mitchell hadn't been charged with any offence in relation to the attack on Bentley, all he could say was that Mitchell had no memory of the incident and he came back 'cured'.

All this was highly unsatisfactory. What was the opinion of the psychiatrists at Haslar? On what grounds was Mitchell released from detention so soon? Was a risk assessment taken in the interests of the prisoner's own health and safety or with a view to the protection of others? Why were no charges pressed against Mitchell? Had Mitchell and Bentley been putting on a mock fight? Had Windsor and Wilson been duped? Answers to some or all of these important questions might have been forthcoming if George Wilson had been available to testify at the inquest, or failing that a doctor from Haslar with knowledge of Mitchell's case. But Edgar Goble felt strongly there was no need to hold up the inquest until Wilson was well enough to testify. He thought the jury had heard enough evidence already.

The inquest hearing was a disgrace. Goble degraded his profession by presiding over proceedings that were confused and full of contradictions. And he failed in his primary duty to fully investigate the circumstances of Margaret Treble's death. The coroner's independence and impartiality can be called into question at almost every stage of the hearing.

In his summing up the coroner told the jury, 'It was certain that poor Mrs Treble met her death from the wound inflicted by the bullet fired by the sailor. The unfortunate man [Mitchell] may have been mentally deranged and was not responsible for what he did at the time'.[70] And so it was that the coroner, who opened proceedings with the unambiguous statement that it was not the job of the court to decide the question of responsibility of a sane or insane man,

70 *Hampshire Post*, 24 August 1906.

ended up declaring that Mitchell was insane and not responsible for his actions at the time he committed murder. But the only testimony touching on Mitchell's mental health and his criminal responsibility came from Dr Cross, who had no professional training in mental pathology and who, in any case, had little acquaintance with the details of Mitchell's case.

Despite repeatedly advising the jury that it was not their job — or indeed the job of the coroner and the witnesses — to speculate on whether Mitchell was *compos mentis*, this didn't stop Goble from bringing up other cases he had dealt with which he thought were of 'a somewhat similar character'. One such case involved a murder on Christmas Day in 1898 at the Browndown rifle ranges, near Gosport.[71] James Whatmore, a private in the Royal Marine Light Infantry, was stabbed to death by a comrade, Lance-Corporal Henry Spurrier, as the two men were sitting in front of the fire in their hut at Browndown Camp. At the trial in Winchester it was stated that Spurrier had likely committed the crime while recovering from an epileptic seizure. He was dazed after the tragedy and had no recollection of the incident. The jury returned a verdict of guilty but insane, and Spurrier was sent to Broadmoor.

Of course, there are superficial similarities between the Mitchell and Spurrier cases, especially regards the determination of memory loss and epileptic mania. But there are crucial differences as well. Spurrier had an extensive family history of insanity and epilepsy — his father, an aunt and an uncle, and a sister were all committed to asylums suffering from epileptic fits — whereas in Mitchell's case there was no verifiable history of insanity in the family;[72] Spurrier was diagnosed as an 'epileptic maniac' by a medical superintendent at the County Lunatic Asylum at Fareham, whereas in Mitchell's case no credible medical diagnosis of mental illness had been presented to the court to support the coroner's view that Mitchell was insane and not responsible for his actions. And nor could there have been because Mitchell was feigning mental illness.

According to the coroner, the jurors had 'no other course open to them than to return a verdict of wilful murder . . . The case was not one of manslaughter, but of downright murder'. The evidence, said the coroner in his summing up, pointed to Mitchell having 'homicidal tendencies'. Technically the coroner left the verdict to the consideration of the jurors, but in effect he directed them to find Mitchell guilty of wilful murder.

Almost as an afterthought, the coroner drew the jury's attention to Dr Cross's theory that Mrs Treble might have survived the shooting if the bullet hadn't struck the clasp of the purse in her pocket. But Goble wasn't interested in the wounding mechanism per se; he had no interest in determining if the injuries suffered by the deceased were feasibly the result of a gunshot wound produced by a Lee-Metford rifle from a distance of under twenty yards. This was just a pretext

71 See *Hampshire Telegraph*, 7 January 1899, for a report of the inquest hearing conducted by Goble; *Hampshire Telegraph*, 14 January 1899, for a report of the committal hearing; *Hampshire Telegraph*, 18 February 1899, for a report of the trial at the Winchester Assizes.
72 Of course, the anonymity of his biological father leaves open the possibility that Mitchell may have inherited tendencies of insanity from his father.

for launching into one of his interminable Napoleonic War anecdotes about how the life of one of the sailors on the poop deck of the *Victory* at Trafalgar had been miraculously saved when a bullet hit a silver watch in his pocket.

As his summing up came to a close, he commented on one aspect of the case that strictly speaking had nothing to do with the death of Margaret Treble. It concerned Fleet Goldsmith and his gunning down of Mitchell outside the Seven Stars in Stroud. While the coroner had nothing but praise for his fellow Mason (he referred to Goldsmith's 'praiseworthy pluck'), he could not say that Goldsmith had acted in an absolutely legal way. His felt his actions were more in keeping with 'what one would find in the backwoods of America'. According to Goble, 'Even if a man did not aim directly at people but shot indiscriminately about populated streets, and thus brought about death, he was liable to be charged with the capital offence.'[73] In other words, if Goldsmith had mortally wounded Mitchell, or if an innocent bystander had died as a result of his actions, his position would have been serious.[74] No doubt Captain Tew, if he was among the spectators in court that Tuesday afternoon, would have felt very uncomfortable at these remarks from the coroner.

It took the jury less than five minutes to reach a verdict of wilful murder against Herbert Mitchell, alias Joseph Burbidge.

*

The funeral of Margaret Treble took place in West Meon on Tuesday afternoon. All of the relatives of the deceased, and many of the witnesses and spectators at the court house, were anxious to conclude business in Petersfield so that they could rush over to St John's church for the service. Goble himself was due to attend a Freemason's lodge meeting in Fareham that evening, so perhaps these two events influenced his decision to bring the inquest to a speedy and premature close.

In a coffin of polished elm Mrs Treble was laid to rest in a quiet corner of the churchyard near to the grave of another member of her family.[75]

> The funeral was attended by practically the whole of the residents of West Meon, as well as by farmers and other well-known people from a long distance round. Every shop was closed and every blind drawn during the

73 *Hampshire Post*, 24 August 1906.
74 In 1906 there were few statutory controls on the carrying and use of firearms. The Vagrancy Act 1824 made it an offence to possess a gun or any other offensive weapon with the intent to commit a felony. The Firearms Act 1920, introduced in response to growing public concern at the proliferation of firearms in private hands after the Great War, was the first wide-ranging piece of legislation to address gun control in England.
75 Thomas Lord (1755–1832), who founded Lord's Cricket Ground, is also buried in the churchyard. Despite opposition from many villagers, the ashes of the Soviet spy Guy Burgess were interred in the family plot at West Meon churchyard in 1963.

> ceremony, and the streets were lined as the church was approached by saddened and mournful groups of people.[76]

Amongst the mourners were Superintendent King and a number of crew from HMS *Nelson*. No one at the funeral realised that Mitchell was actually a native of Hampshire, having been born fewer that thirty miles away in the small village of Nether Wallop.

76 *Hants and Sussex News*, 29 August 1906.

21. Cricket match (*Hampshire Post*, 31 August 1906) *Copyright the British Library Board*

22. *Left* Margaret Treble (*Weekly Dispatch*, 2 September 1906) 23. *Right* Margaret Treble (*Hampshire Post*, 24 August 1906) *Both copyright the British Library Board*

24. *Left* Doris and Minnie Mitchell, early 1960s. 25. Doris Mitchell in 1939. 26. Doris Mitchell, early 1960s. *All three by kind permission of Judy Gibbons and Hannah Chandler*

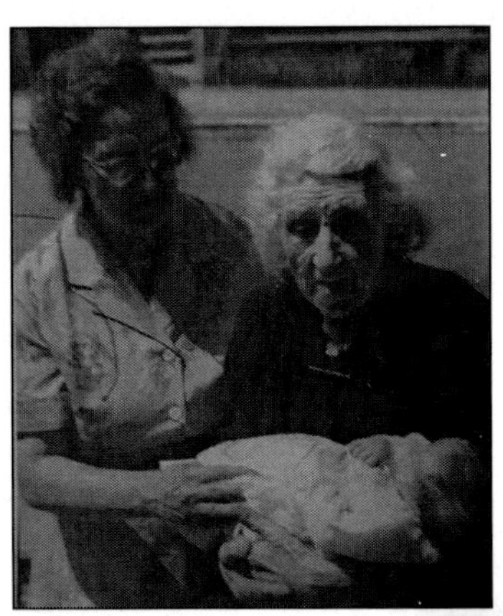

27. Picture postcard of bullet and casing found in Petersfield (Louis Hayward 1906). *Provided by Petersfield Museum Limited PTFPM:2012.601*

28. *Left* Mr Justice Kennedy, c.1915. *Private collection*

29. *Right* John Simon, 1st Viscount Simon, c.1916, prosecuting counsel at Mitchell's trial and later Home Secretary. *Private collection*

30. Winchester Great Hall where Mitchell stood trial. *Private collection*

31. Broadmoor Asylum entrance, 1908. *Copyright the Francis Frith Collection*

5

'Tales of demonology'

Nether Wallop is situated about eight miles south-west of Andover, close to the border with Wiltshire. It is predominantly a farming community, surrounded by wheat and barley fields, water meadows, beech woods and plantations. The Iron Age hill fort of Danebury Ring lies a few miles to the east on the way to Stockbridge. A narrow lane connects Nether Wallop to Middle Wallop and Over Wallop. Across the fields, about three miles north-west of the parish, is Grateley railway station on the London to Exeter line of the London and South Western Railway. There is a church, two pubs (although The Five Bells is closed at the time of writing), a cluster of shops, and a village school. It is considered one of the prettiest villages in Hampshire.

Usually not much happens in the village. In 1844 Mr Thomas Coombs of Nether Wallop exhibited his new universal corn and turnip drill at the Southampton Agricultural Show. In January 1885, Ethel Toomer, aged one year, died of her injuries when a benzoline lamp tipped over and set her clothing aflame.[77] In 1886, Edward Silver was fatally thrown from his horse while driving a cart laden with hay;[78] and that same year Arthur Leonine of Middle Wallop jumped into the sea off Brighton with a heavy bag of sand and pebbles tied to his feet.[79] And it was here, on 9 October 1883, that Herbert Cyril John Mitchell was born.[80]

His mother, Elizabeth Mitchell (*née* Alding), and her husband James, were domestic servants working at Garlogs, a large three storied seventeen bedroom manor house standing in its own parks and woodland on the road between Nether Wallop and Broughton. The mansion was approached by a long carriage drive; at the rear of the property there was a fish pond, a summer house, and a walled kitchen garden, together with stabling for eight horses and other outbuildings. In total there were more than twenty servants taking care of the estate.

Belita Jepson-Turner, the Olympic ice skater and Hollywood actress (known to her fans as 'Belita — the Ice Maiden') was born at Garlogs in 1923, and she has left us a fascinating memoir of her childhood in Nether Wallop in the nineteen twenties and thirties:

> There were always house parties and visitors, of course during the shooting and hunting season huge luncheons and balls . . . Daddy even carried his gun to church on Sundays in case he saw vermin that he could kill on the

77 *Hampshire Chronicle*, 10 January 1885.
78 'Fatal accident', *Hampshire Chronicle*, 11 September 1886.
79 'Extraordinary suicide at Brighton', *Hampshire Chronicle*, 24 July 1886.
80 The admission document in Mitchell's Broadmoor case file incorrectly records his date of birth as 19 October 1883. D/H14/02/2/1/2157

way. He did not dare take the gun in during a service so he would prop it up in the portal before entering. I remember seeing the gun and thinking how odd it looked standing there . . . We rarely used the front staircase, it was much nicer to use the back stairs behind the baize door. These led, by way of the servants' passage, to the stable courtyard, then past the garages and under the arch with the old clock, to the stables and dairy, past these up some stone stairs to freedom. Miles of fields and woods with no grown ups.[81]

She had a room entirely given over to her 300 dolls. 'It was a strange, dark little room and the jackdaws were always falling down the chimney, giving it an eerie feeling.'[82]

In the 560 acre grounds there were six farms and several lodges and cottages providing tied accommodation for the staff. The Mitchells lived alongside the cowman and one of the gardeners in The Lodge, an ornamental detached property bordering the Wallop Brook. James was employed mainly as a coachman, although over the years he seems to have lent his hand to a variety of other tasks around the estate. He may have tended the lawns and flowerbeds, and helped out in the stables. Much later he became a groom.

Space was tight at The Lodge, and family members tended to move out when they reached fourteen. In 1881 the eldest child, Elizabeth (19), was working as a domestic servant in Kensington. Fanny (17) was also in service at nearby Berry Court Farm, while George (15) helped out on the Garlogs estate as a shepherd boy and agricultural labourer. The younger children, William (13), Frances (9) and Selina (7), all attended the village school. Charlotte, the fifth daughter, came along the following year in 1882.

Herbert was the youngest member of the family. There is no father's name on his birth certificate, indicating that Herbert was an illegitimate child. Presumably his mother had Herbert by a man other than her husband. The birth was registered on 26 November 1883. Interestingly, the child's name on the certificate is Hubert Cyril John rather than Herbert Cyril John — a name Herbert would revert to in later life.

Little is known of Herbert's background prior to his enlisting in the Royal Navy in 1903. It is possible that James and Elizabeth Mitchell brought up Herbert as if he was their joint offspring, in which case we can surmise that he, too, attended the village school like his half-brothers and sisters. He may even have participated in the celebrations for the Queen's Jubilee in 1887. In the blazing sunshine there was a procession of 120 children through the village, followed by afternoon tea in the meadows and a sporting gala (Mrs Toomer won the 100 yards

81 Available online at https://skateguard1.blogspot.com/2017/06/all-best-belita-definitive-biography-of.html

82 During the Second World War Garlogs was requisitioned by the RAF as accommodation for the special duty clerks who worked shifts in the Operations Room at Middle Wallop Fighter-Bomber station. The owner of the house, retired Major Jepson-Turner, was ejected from his home and forced to slum it in the gardener's cottage. See Patricia Margaret, *No Wonder I Like Butterflies: A Life of Travel* (Matador, 2013), pp.26.

race for women over 20 and under 40). The children were given presents of toys, work baskets, and pocket knives! In the evening there was a fireworks display and dancing in the park for adults.[83]

But it is far more likely that Herbert was given up for adoption. The fact that there is no trace of Herbert in the 1891 census, and that his whereabouts are a complete mystery until his late teens, suggests strongly that Herbert was taken away from Nether Wallop in his infant years and brought up under the name of his adoptive parents. In 1893 the school leaving age was raised to 11, so it is likely that Mitchell, wherever he went to school, was kept on for at least an additional year.

Sometime in the late 1890s Mitchell may have been accepted at one of the Admiralty-run training ships that prepared boys to go to sea as signallers. These establishments were usually old warships that had come to the end of their active service and were converted into classrooms and dormitories. The nearest one was the brig HMS *St Vincent* at Haslar. Recruits were generally accepted between the ages of fifteen and sixteen and-a-half so long as their parents gave consent. The candidates had to pass a medical examination as well as an academic assessment — the ability to read and write was essential. Usually basic training lasted between nine and fifteen months, producing at the end of it boys of good education with the requisite skills to go to sea as telegraphists and signallers.

In 1900 the British Navy was on the verge of adopting wireless telegraphy as the universally accepted system of signalling throughout the service. Military telegraphists were therefore becoming increasingly in demand, especially in the Mediterranean where the British Fleet patrolled the trade routes between Britain and India.

One of the vessels sent to the Mediterranean at this time was the 20 knot cruiser HMS *Pyramus.* It was commissioned for active service in April 1900 with a complement of 230 men under the command of John de Robeck. It set sail from Sheerness on 11 June and arrived at Gibraltar on the 18th, reaching Malta four days later. On board, supposedly, was boy signaller Herbert Mitchell, although no service records exist to verify this claim. Our only source for this early seafaring adventure comes from Mitchell himself in his statements to Dr Cross at Petersfield police station and Dr McGregor at Kingston prison. If he enlisted on *Pyramus* he will have done so under his adopted name, or a variation of it.

In Malta there was time for a cricket match at Corradino on a pitch made of cement covered by cocoa-nut matting[84] before *Pyramus* sailed to Suda Bay (Crete) in August. In early October it cruised to the Turkish city of Smyrna (now Izmir) on the Aegean coast, later rejoining the fleet at Malta in mid-November. By then, though, it appears Mitchell was no longer among the crew.

At the inquest Dr Cross recited Mitchell's account of what had happened at sea:

83 'Jubilee Celebration', *Salisbury and Winchester Journal*, 16 July 1887.
84 HMS *Pyramus* defeated HMS *Dryad* by 28 runs, Captain de Robeck scoring a 'dashing 52'. See 'Cricket at Malta', *Cambridge Daily News*, 12 July 1900.

At the port of Saigon[85] he had a severe sunstroke. He said he was detained in hospital from three to four months, during most of which time he had to be under restraint, owing, witness presumed, to his not being in his right mind. He had procured a passage home and then joined the Navy under his real name.

Throughout his life, Mitchell would experience bouts of depression and melancholia during the summer months, all of which he put down to that first crippling spell of sunstroke on the Turkish coast. Yet even if the symptoms were as severe as he reported, surely he will have been cared for by the medical team on *Pyramus* or by staff at the British Seamen's Hospital at Smyrna, and then brought back to England. Mitchell's picaresque tale of being disembarked and abandoned in a Turkish hospital or asylum for several months, and then making his own way back to England without any money, sounds frankly far-fetched.[86]

*

Back in England, homeless and out of work, Herbert will probably have made his way to the Sydenham Hill and Lewisham area of south-east London where he had family connections. His oldest half-sister, Elizabeth, had left Nether Wallop sometime before her nineteenth birthday to work as a domestic servant in Kensington. While in London, she met George Ansett, an army soldier born and raised in Sydenham. They married in 1888 then moved to Jersey when George got posted to Fort Regent in St Helier. By 1901 they were back in Sydenham, living at 43 Miall Road with their first five children (Elizabeth would go on to have nine children in 25 years). According to the 1901 census, someone called Frederick Millar, a 35-year-old bricklayer and labourer from Crawley in Sussex was staying with the family on the night of March 31. He is listed as the brother of the head of the family, which is plainly untrue. Could this have been Herbert Mitchell, bedding down at his half-sister's home while he got his life together?

Around 1901 Mitchell met Minnie Amelia Martin. She resided at 41 Knighton Park Road in Lewisham with a Mr Charles Passingham and his wife Alice. On the 1901 census her occupation is given as mother's help, suggesting she might have looked after the two Passingham children, Dorothy and Edward, in return for board.[87] Born in Devonport in 1873, she grew up in Stoke Damerel; her mother died when she was only twelve years old, and she moved to London in her early twenties. Not a great deal is known about her relationship with Herbert, but it seems around January 1902 Minnie became pregnant with Herbert's child. Almost certainly, Herbert and Minnie married that same year, although the marriage

85 Early newspaper reports incorrectly gave Saigon as Mitchell's destination — perhaps this was originally an error by Cross; naval records clearly show that *Pyramus* was in Smyrna in October 1900.
86 For contemporary theories on insanity and sunstroke, see Theo B. Hyslop, 'Sunstroke and Insanity', in *Journal of Mental Science*, October 1890, pp.494–504.
87 RG 13/557 page 14.

certificate has not yet surfaced, and it is always possible they lived together as man and wife. Minnie was actually ten years older than Herbert. In November, Albert Slade was born.

Mitchell continued looking for work. Ideally, he wanted to enlist in the Royal Navy. Towards the end of 1903 an opportunity presented itself, and on September 30 he signed up as a 2nd class stoker aboard HMS *Nelson.*

Launched in 1874, *Nelson* was a steel-hulled armoured cruiser. It had served as the flagship of the British naval command in Australian and New Zealand waters before becoming a guardship at Portsmouth in 1891. Eleven years later it was hulked and refitted as a training ship for stokers at Portsmouth dockyard.

Mitchell joined for 12 years under the false name Charles Mitchell. He also lied about his date and place of birth, which is recorded on his service papers as '5th July 1883 — Andover, Hants'. His previous occupation is given as fireman (the term for stoker used in the merchant navy). He was one month short of twenty; 5 ft 7½in tall, black hair, brown eyes, dark complexion. He had a number of tattoos: a ship on his left bicep, a star on his left forearm, a basket of flowers on his right bicep, a coat of arms on his right forearm, a sailor and woman's head on his left shin.[88] On the first day he joined he was supplied with his free kit — one pair of fearnought trousers, one canvas suit, and one pair of boots.

*

For most of his short career at sea, Mitchell toiled in the boiler and engine rooms of ocean-going steamships.

It was the job of a stoker or a fireman to tend the coal fires for the running of boilers that powered the screw propellers that drove the ships. HMS *Nelson* had ten oval boilers fuelling a pair of three-cylinder steam engines, each driving a single propeller. Coal was stored in bunkers strategically located around the ship; the coal was humped in wheelbarrows to the stokehold, and from there shovelled into the fireboxes of the boiler furnaces. Temperatures in the boiler room could reach 160 degrees Fahrenheit.

The authors of *Ocean Steamships* describe conditions in the bowels of the vessel:

> The engine-rooms and stoke-holes of a great steamer are forbidden ground, are lands *taboo*, save to those specially asked to visit them . . . When you come to measure the region fairly, it broadens into a wonder-land: it shapes itself into a twilight island of mysteries, into a laboratory where grimy alchemists practise black magic and white . . . Under the splintering silver of the electric lamps . . . figures nearly naked, gritty and black with coal, and pasty with ashes, and soaked with sweat, come and go in the blazing light and in the half gloom, and seem like nightmares from fantastic tales of demonology.[89]

88 His service number was SS 305021. See ADM 188/497.
89 F. E. Chadwick, et al., *Ocean Steamships* (New York: Charles Scribner's Sons, 1891), pp.170–72.

It was unbelievably arduous work — a large ship could consume upwards of 1,000 tons of coal a day. And dangerous, too: boilers and steam pipes might explode, ejecting scalding water and burning debris over the men, and there was the ever-present risk of lung disease from inhaling coal dust particles. Generally, stokers worked for four hours at a stretch, attending to four furnaces; a man might be occupied at each furnace for about three minutes, after which he would rush to the airpipe and wait until his turn came round again.[90] Robert Machray paints a vivid picture of the lot of a fireman/stoker:

> There is no man who sails the sea who has so bad a time as the fireman: his work brutalises him; the heat in the interior of the steamboats drives him mad: his thirst is quenchless — he goes to sea nearly always drunk — he wakes from his stupor with a raging thirst — he remains thirsty — when he gets ashore he rushes to the nearest drinking-den to quench that awful thirst of his. He is poorly paid, and what he receives on landing, at most two or three pounds, soon disappears: it melts in a few hours; usually it is stolen from him; he never really gives himself a chance, nor does anyone else give him one.[91]

In fact, the range of duties and skills required of a stoker were far greater than Machray suggests. The old Scotch fire-tube boilers of a generation before were being replaced by water-tube boilers whose furnaces were fed by oil fuel as well as coal; marine engines were evolving into complex petrol, gas and electrical machines. The man behind the shovel needed to keep abreast of all these developments.

Stokers also took part in landing/boarding parties – they were notoriously rough and rowdy members of crew who frequently engaged in fights with each other or with natives on shore, or both.[92]

Additionally, since the 1890s stokers were increasingly drilled in the same way as ordinary seamen. As part of their basic training, stokers received instruction in firearms and field craft from the Gunnery Staff of the ships in which they served. Stokers who passed the examination in Field Training received 1d a day extra pay on top of their regular remuneration of one shilling and eight pence.[93]

Basic training lasted five months. Mitchell seems to have completed his training without incident. Indeed, his service papers note that his conduct was

90 'A stoker's work', *Portsmouth Evening News*, 26 December 1905.
91 Robert Machray, *The Night Side of London* (Philadelphia: J.B. Lippincott Company, 1902), p.52.
92 The popular boys' periodical *Chums* (1892–1932) carried a rather fanciful piece on naval stokers entitled 'Amongst the Machinery' (1904): 'The stoker has to know how to wield lethal weapons as well as a coal shovel. On the parade ground every morning you may see squads of them fighting merry duels with single-sticks, or doing "cut and thrust" with the straight-bladed navy cutlass, a weapon that is usable for splitting skulls or firewood.' See *Mid Sussex Times*, 8 March 1904.
93 *The King's Regulations and Admiralty Instructions for the Government of His Majesty's Naval Service 1906* [article 884].

'very good'. Yet like most new entry 2nd class stokers, Mitchell was actually inexperienced at performing even the most basic tasks required in the boiler rooms: these skills had to be learnt quickly 'on the job' while at sea. And like a small minority of all new recruits, Mitchell was an awkward character, surly and short-tempered, and unwilling to knuckle down to service discipline.

Mitchell must have taken weekend leave in November 1903 because that month Minnie became pregnant again with Herbert's second child. The circumstances are confusing and uncertain, but it is clear that Herbert failed to contribute financially to the upbringing of his children. Mitchell's relations with Minnie were always strained and often violent: many years later Minnie would tell the Broadmoor authorities that her husband 'was subject to furious outbursts of temper and ill-used her".[94]

On 3 February 1904 Mitchell was drafted straight from *Nelson* to the commissioned battleship HMS *Hannibal.*

Hannibal had a colourful recent history. On 17 October 1903, while undergoing night-time manoeuvres off Ferrol, Spain, she had collided with and badly damaged her sister ship HMS *Prince George.* Earlier that year, she had been selected to take part in the first trial of fuel oil in a coal-fired engine: on 26 June 1903 she steamed out of Portsmouth Harbour burning coal, switched to oil, and moments later became engulfed in a pall of dense black smoke as a result of faulty burners.

Her departure from Portsmouth to join the Channel fleet was delayed owing to continued problems with the installation of the oil fuel fittings, but on 12 February she assembled at Portland and finally set sail for Vigo on the 18th, arriving there on the 21st.

In theory it was an exciting time to be a stoker: plans to replace coal with oil in the boilers of naval vessels would fundamentally reduce the reliance on the brawn of stokers transporting and shovelling coal day and night. While 2nd class stokers (the lowest rank of marine engineer rating) inevitably started out as shovellers of coal, for men who showed aptitude and ambition there were increasing opportunities to progress up the career ladder by taking on ever more involved roles such as fire fighting, stowage, and maintaining and operating auxiliary machinery.

Mitchell, however, remained sullen, insubordinate, and quarrelsome throughout the voyage to Vigo. There appears to have been a grudge or a history of ill-feeling between himself and one of his superior officers, which culminated in Mitchell striking the officer with a weapon. At the inquest hearing into Margaret Treble's death, Dr Cross offered the opinion that Mitchell had lashed out at his commanding officer while under the influence of post-epileptic mania:

94 D/H14/02/2/1/2157. Letter from Superintendent Baker to Under Secretary of State at Home Office, 17 February 1916.

When on board the Hannibal in the port of Vigo, in 1904, during one of these fits that he had he went for one of his mates with a spanner, and hit him over the head.[95]

Cross provided no evidence whatsoever to support the claim that Mitchell was an epileptic prone to erratic, aggressive seizures. It makes more sense to view the incident simply as a long-running disagreement between a stoker and his commanding officer that boiled over into physical violence.

HMS *Hannibal* sailed to Lisbon on 22 February, then on to Gibraltar. It was at Gibraltar, on 21 March 1904, that Mitchell was tried by court-martial. He faced seven charges:

First and *seventh*. Using insulting language and behaving with contempt to his Superior Officer. *Second*. Striking with a weapon his Superior Officer, being in the execution of his office. *Third*. Attempting to strike with a weapon his Superior Officer, being in the execution of his office. *Fourth*. Attempting to strike his Superior Officer, being in the execution of his office. *Fifth*. Behaving with contempt to his Superior Officer. *Sixth*. Act to the prejudice of good order and naval discipline in having a weapon concealed on his person.[96]

The first charge was not proved, but he was convicted on all the remaining charges. He was sentenced to two years' civil imprisonment with hard labour at Dorchester prison and then dismissed from His Majesty's Service.

*

In the end, Mitchell served twenty-two months. Presumably he earned a remission of a portion of his sentence for good conduct. On his release in January 1906, he made his way to south-east London to see Minnie and his baby daughter, Doris, who had been born while he was in prison.[97]

Hoping to capitalise on his newly-acquired skills, he found a job as an engine fitter at a motor garage in Lower Sydenham, possibly F. E. Cox & Duffin, who had a garage at 58 Kirkdale, Sydenham.[98] However, things didn't quite work out. According to Dr Cross's testimony at the inquest:

He became employed at a motor garage in Lower Sydenham, but there he soon had another of these fits, and, in his own words, he 'cleared a street'. How he did it I do not know. He said they would not take him back at the garage.[99]

95 *Hampshire Chronicle*, 25 August 1906.
96 ADM 194/185.
97 Doris Kathleen Mitchell was born at 2.20 a.m. on 4 August, 1904. At the time Minnie was living at 23 Stanton Square in Sydenham. The birth was registered on 14 September.
98 An order of adjudication of bankruptcy against the owners was taken out by the County Court in January 1909. See *Kentish Mercury*, 29 January 1909.
99 *Hampshire Chronicle*, 25 August 1906. A witness at the trial would later claim Mitchell had used 'a

There are no reports in any of the local newspapers of a lone male 'clearing a street' or running amok in Sydenham, although on 17 March a seaman from Chatham ran amok down the Edgware Road, 'striking at everyone he met'.[100] Quite possibly Mitchell invented or exaggerated the episode (along with the sham seizure). Dr Cross once again found himself an unsuspecting party to deceit.

Almost certainly, Mitchell was sacked from Cox & Duffin within a couple of months of starting work there. Perhaps there were discipline issues at the garage and continuing arguments with Minnie at home that affected his work. At any rate, he took the decision to re-enlist in the Royal Navy as a stoker using a false name. Of course, having already been discharged with ignominy, he was prohibited from re-enlisting. It was especially brazen to re-join the service knowing full well he would be enrolled at the same ship (HMS *Nelson*) where he had completed his original basic training just over two years previously. He must have felt confident he wouldn't be recognised by any of the regular officers or long-serving instructors.

On 3 April 1906 he signed up as a 2nd class stoker. Once more he was supplied with his free kit — one pair of fearnought trousers, one canvas suit, and one pair of boots. As before, he joined for twelve years. On this occasion, though, he used the name Joseph Burbidge. (Mitchell was a man of many identities — Hubert Mitchell, Herbert Mitchell, Charles Mitchell, Frederick Millar, Joseph Burbidge.) His service papers wrongly give the date and place of birth as '1 June 1883 — Sydenham, Kent'. Previous occupation is listed as engine fitter. He was six months short of twenty-three; 5 ft 7½in tall, dark hair, brown eyes, dark complexion. Miraculously, his tattoos had shifted position since his last period of service: the basket of flowers had moved from the right bicep to the left forearm, the woman's head had switched from the left shin to the right arm, the coat of arms on the right forearm had vanished altogether. The only consistent distinguishing mark across the two terms or service was the star on his left forearm.[101]

Mitchell had already sailed through his basic training in 1903–04. Repeating the same exercises and drills and attending the same lectures two years later must have been a doddle. He knew his way around; he knew how things worked. He began to exploit situations to his own advantage. No doubt he had a head start on all the other recruits and was able to make plans for the stealing of ammunition from the Tipner firing range. Yet certain matters preyed on him. For one thing, he convinced himself he had contracted venereal disease:

> When I contracted ghonerhea [*sic*] I did not know what to do with myself, it having come to the knowledge of my friends and my shipmates. I could not stand the ridicule. In addition to this I had contracted some debts which I was unable to meet.[102]

broom handle and a poker'.
100 'A bluejacket runs amok', *Portsmouth Evening News*, 20 March 1906.
101 His service number was SS 309961. See ADM 188/506.
102 D/H14/02/2/1/2157 Statement from Herbert C. J. Mitchell to Superintendent Brayn, 7 May 1907. His medical records at Winchester Prison and Broadmoor give no indication of gonorrheal infection.

Mitchell was becoming increasingly gloomy and irascible. He began to feel trapped within the suffocating atmosphere of the barracks, oppressed by what he saw as petty military regulations. He realised now he had made a terrible mistake in signing away his life for twelve years with the Royal Navy. At some point he settled on a plan to secure his 'freedom'.

> I then tried to get sent away from the ship to another ship, but failed. Then I tried to get invalided from the service. I started by feigning fainting fits and attempts at suicide, but nobody said anything about it as I was getting on well at my training.[103]

However, one of his 'suicide attempts' on 19 July *did* attract the attention of the authorities. This was the Harry Bentley incident described in an earlier chapter. Mitchell's own account of this affair, and his subsequent hospitalisation at Haslar, is worth quoting in full:

> One night I procured a razor and a bottle of black wash, and went to the latrine. I was sitting on the seat when a shipmate named Bentley came in to the place. He tried to take the things away from me and I struggled with him. Next morning the doctor sent me over to Haslar hospital where I was detained a fortnight. I [was] discharged as cured from mental disease. The ghonerhea [*sic*] had also been cured in the meantime and I thought I should be able to carry on alright again.[104]

We need to be cautious about accepting Mitchell's words at face value. His version of events is to some extent a self-serving statement, intended to manipulate the Broadmoor authorities into moving him away from a block housing dangerous and violent patients into a facility reserved for low-risk, trustworthy patients. In addition, Mitchell may have been concerned to protect Bentley by not implicating him as a confederate in his ruse to dupe the naval authorities.

In essence, Mitchell's scheme was to obtain a discharge from the Navy on compassionate grounds by faking suicidal thoughts and feigning 'fainting fits'. It was a risky strategy: while stokers were regularly invalided as a result of accidents and physical injuries sustained on or off duty, they were rarely discharged on account of mental aberration or psychological distress. It is important to note that Mitchell did not seek to simulate epileptic seizures *per se* — he didn't know anything at all about the condition, and later expressed surprise that Dr Cross and the doctors in charge at Winchester prison were interpreting his sham fits as epileptic in origin. Rather, he cobbled together a series of behaviours or symptoms he intuitively felt might convince the authorities of his mental illness — he fell to the floor, writhed about on the ground for a while, went into a pretend stupor, and afterwards falsely claimed memory loss. It was only later,

103 D/H14/02/2/1/2157 Statement from Herbert C. J. Mitchell to Superintendent Brayn, 7 May 1907.
104 Ibid.

once the doctors had started labelling his 'fits' as epileptic and suggesting to him that his violent outbursts were the consequence of post-epileptic mania, that he began reporting symptoms in line with their diagnosis. In this way he was able to concoct an entirely fictitious but convincing history of chronic 'mental illness' that hoodwinked the authorities. None of the doctors examining Mitchell had witnessed their patient experiencing a petit mal attack or a major fit; they were totally dependent on Mitchell's own accounts of his supposed seizures. The sunstroke in Smyrna and the use of hospital restraints, the officer attacked with a spanner in Vigo, the 'street clearing' incident in Sydenham, the attack with a razor on Bentley aboard the *Nelson* — all these dramatic events, invented, exaggerated, embellished, or taken out of context, became components of a manufactured seven-year history of seizures accompanied by outbursts of violence and memory loss that somehow convinced the doctors their prisoner suffered from post-epileptic homicidal mania.

No one could have been more surprised than Mitchell when, after a fortnight's observation on the 'maniac's ward' at Haslar hospital, he was given a clean bill of health and discharged cured from hospital. On 2 August he was escorted back to HMS *Nelson*, where he was seen by a medical officer next morning, pronounced rational, and returned immediately to active duty. He fully expected to be punished for his 'affray' with Bentley, but to his amazement nothing more was said about the incident. Mitchell was learning not only how simple it was to fake mental illness and fool the doctors, but how effortless it was afterwards to be 'cured' and to suffer no repercussions for his actions.

An internal inquiry conducted by the Admiralty would later look into the question of why Mitchell was released from Haslar hospital so soon after he had supposedly attacked a shipmate with a razor. There is no real mystery, though. What seems to have happened is that staff at Haslar were unable to find anything wrong with Mitchell, hence they assumed his ailment, malady, disorder — whatever it was — had gone into remission. Apparently they never seriously contemplated the possibility that Mitchell (who hadn't attacked anyone with a razor) was malingering. George Wilson, the medical officer attached to HMS *Nelson*, was himself malingering to avoid attending the inquest to give evidence about his own disastrous role in the Mitchell affair.

Mitchell must have wondered what more he could do to get himself signed off as mentally ill from the Navy. On the evening of 12 August he half-heartedly threw another 'fit' while walking between Unicorn Gate and his ship, but his mess-mates, by now used to Mitchell's antics, simply picked him up and carried him aboard as if he were drunk.

As Mitchell tells the story, it was a shipmate who first put the idea of 'running amok' into his head:

> I started feigning fits again when a shipmate in a joke told me it was no good carrying on that way but I ought to pretend to shoot somebody. I acted on his idea. I procured between 30 to 40 rounds of ammunition . . .[105]

105 D/H14/02/2/1/2157 Statement from Herbert C. J. Mitchell to Superintendent Brayn, 7 May 1907.

*

Running amok in the streets and injuring everybody within reach was hardly a new phenomenon. Indeed, on the very day that the inquest jury committed Mitchell for trial at the Winchester Assizes, an on-duty Liverpool policeman drew his truncheon and for no good reason started lashing out at members of the public, striking right and left, and causing severe injuries. The day before, a barman had gone berserk through the streets of Paddington attacking passers-by with a hockey stick.[106]

Incidents such as these were popularly associated in the public imagination with Malay and Indonesian cultures, and with native soldiers in the Indian Empire.[107] In common usage the term 'running amok' simply refers to an individual acting irrationally and causing havoc, but in the psychiatric literature *amok* is defined as a 'culture-specific syndrome wherein an individual unpredictably and without warning manifests mass, indiscriminate, homicidal behaviour that is authored with suicidal intent'.[108] Historically, the typical perpetrator was a young Malay man:

> In 1901, in the province of Phang, Malaysia, a 23-year-old Muslim man who was formerly a member of the police force stole a Malay sword and attacked 5 individuals while they were sleeping or smoking opium. He killed 3, almost decapitating 1 victim, and he seriously wounded the others.[109]

So frequent were *amok* attacks that as recently as August 1905 Lord Kitchener had issued instructions to all ranks of the Indian Army on how to deal with 'armed men who are smitten with sudden frenzy and run amok':

> If possible, they are to be captured and placed carefully in custody, but in cases where the man cannot be captured and his prolonged liberty is a menace to the safety of the community he must, if circumstances warrant such a step, be shot down.[110]

Mitchell settled on a less-violent form of *amok*. He would march through the streets deliberately firing *above* people's heads and aiming *away* from crowds. His object was to frighten and scare — 'terrorise' is the best word for it — but not to cause physical injury. By combining this *amok* strategy with his tried and tested 'fainting fit' routine, he imagined he would be taken into custody for causing alarm and distress in public and placed under observation in a hospital somewhere. After a week or two, he could then magically 'recover' his sanity (as

106 'Two men run amok', *Herts & Cambs Reporter*, 24 August 1906.
107 *'Amok'* is derived from the Malay word 'mengamok', which means to make a furious and desperate charge.
108 J. C. Spores, *Running Amok: An Historical Inquiry* (Athens, OH, 1988), p.7.
109 B. G. Burton-Bradley, 'The amok syndrome in Papua and New Guinea', *Medical Journal of Australia* 1(7) (1968), pp.252–256.
110 *Salisbury Times*, 4 August 1905.

he'd done at Haslar), the Navy would discharge him, and he would be free to do whatever he wanted. That was the master plan. Perhaps the finer details of the scheme hadn't been fully worked out in his mind. What if he was court-martialed for breaking away from Tipner with a loaded firearm? What if members of the public started returning fire? And certainly, he couldn't have foreseen that he would be indicted for the murder of a member of the public who had died from a shot fired by someone else.

There is a real sense that Mitchell's planned 'shooting spree' was common knowledge among recruits at the *Nelson* barracks. There may have been dark rumours circulating that he was plotting a deliberate act of terror. Perhaps Mitchell had spoken openly about his intentions but in a vague, boastful sort of way that made his shipmates shrug off his threats as 'wild' talk. When he joined the other stokers for firearms training at Tipner, there was banter about Mitchell's state of mind: the instructor, Henry Birch, knew that Mitchell had recently been on the sick list, and on Monday morning before class he asked him if he was well enough to take part in the training sessions. 'You won't be shooting anybody, will you?' he joked.

Almost certainly, Mitchell enlisted the assistance of one or two of his shipmates to help smuggle ammunition out of Tipner, and on Friday, when he asked permission to use the latrine at Tipner and never returned, his absence must have been noticed by his comrades yet they chose not to say anything to senior officers at the firing range.

At the Crown trial, Dr McGregor from Portsmouth prison offered the opinion that Mitchell experienced an epileptic fit while sitting on the latrine; according to McGregor, this 'fit' precipitated the eight-hour fugue and the subsequent violent behaviour at Petersfield. But this is nonsense. Mitchell had planned the attack days ahead. He'd come prepared with money, he'd already smuggled ammunition and secured the rifle *before* he visited the latrine. Nipping to the toilets was an excuse to break away from his comrades at the firing range and scarper over the fields. Even so, we have to wonder why Mitchell never considered executing his shooting spree in (say) Stamshaw village rather than traipsing fifteen miles over the countryside to reach Petersfield, a town he had never previously visited.

Feigning memory loss was a key part of Mitchell's plan. It had proved effective in the past, enabling Mitchell to avoid answering tricky questions from the police and hospital staff. Having no memory for a particular crime tended to suggest, moreover, that the act was to some extent impulsive or not premeditated, which served to mitigate criminal responsibility. However, the drawback of fabricating amnesia soon became apparent to Mitchell — by claiming he had no recollections of his activities at Petersfield, he found he was unable to refute the accusation that he had murdered Margaret Treble. The charge of murder was so pervasive and so pernicious that even Mitchell ended up half-believing he had fired the bullet that killed Mrs Treble:

> One of the [bullets] had unfortunately struck the woman, which proved fatal. I was not aware of this until next morning when the police told me

and charged me with it. How this shot struck her I am unable to say, unless it was a ~~richo~~ ricochet. I am a remarkably good shot with a rifle and if that was my intention I could have made every shot tell, but I was only firing over their heads. I cannot tell how it happened. I could not believe it at first and thought they were joking.[111]

Mitchell's best option in this situation would have been to come clean about his feigned memory loss. The prosecution case was so dire even a half-competent defence barrister might have secured Mitchell's acquittal on the murder charge. But Mitchell was unrepresented at the magistrates' court, he was receiving poor advice outside of it, and forces were gathering that would inevitably ensure a wrongful conviction.

111 D/H14/02/2/1/2157 Statement from Herbert C. J. Mitchell to Superintendent Brayn, 7 May 1907.

6

Committal hearing

After his brief initial appearance before the magistrates on Saturday 17 August, Mitchell was escorted to Kingston prison in Portsmouth, where he was placed under the care of medical officer Dr James McGregor. The prison doctor examined Mitchell on Sunday morning, finding him 'dull and depressed' and with no memory of the offence in Petersfield. (Mitchell, of course, was feigning amnesia.) McGregor questioned him about his past, and Mitchell volunteered the tales he had told Dr Cross the day before — sunstroke in Smyrna, the 'assault' aboard HMS *Hannibal*, the Sydenham *amok*. Alarmed at what he was hearing, McGregor ordered Mitchell to be put in a padded cell for his own protection and presumably for the safety of others in the prison. He was kept in the padded cell the whole time he was at Kingston, and 'specially watched both night and day'.

McGregor had conducted a fairly listless and perfunctory examination and showed himself no more capable of detecting factitious illness than Dr Cross. On the flimsiest of evidence he concurred with Cross that Mitchell was of unsound mind and an epileptic maniac. Mitchell's confinement in a padded cell was a wholly unnecessary precaution, which served only to intensify the notion that Mitchell was an arch-villain and a dangerous lunatic.

Mitchell seems to have received no visitors while at Kingston other than medical staff and the Admiralty Law Agent at Portsmouth, Mr E. J. Harvey, who was overseeing the civil custody arrangements on behalf of the Admiralty. According to Mitchell, he did manage to unburden himself to someone (possibly the prison chaplain, Rev C. T. Rolfe), who seems, however, to have merely encouraged Mitchell in his doomed course of action:

> [At Kingston] I made up my mind to say nothing. I told one person the true facts of the case and he advised me to hold my tongue, telling me I would be alright.[112]

*

On Friday 24 August Mitchell was brought back to Petersfield for the adjourned magistrates' hearing. He arrived at the railway station at a quarter to ten, in handcuffs and escorted by two warders from Kingston. As he was walking up the platform, he was recognised by a party of sailors travelling in the same train: they crowded to the window and shouted out a few cheery comments. Mitchell nodded and smiled in response.

112 D/H14/02/2/1/2157 Statement from Herbert C. J. Mitchell to Superintendent Brayn, 7 May 1907.

The *Hampshire Chronicle* carried a detailed description of the accused man:

> He is a tall, muscularly built man, inclined, if anything, to be lanky rather than stout. His features are not bad, but he is somewhat sallow-complexioned, and there comes into his eyes at times a sad, half-dazed expression, and a look as though his thoughts were elsewhere than upon what is passing before him. Outwardly, he conducted himself as a rational, self-possessed man. For a time he stood straight-up at attention in the dock, with his hands behind him, sailor fashion. Then when he tired, for he was kept standing in the dock the whole two-and-a-half hours the proceedings lasted, he would fold his arms and his tattooed wrists and hands again bespoke the sailor. He smiled across at a mess-mate in Court, and while for the most part he was listening to what the witnesses had to say he once evidently wearied of it, and turned aside to read a printed bill at the end of the dock near where he was standing.
>
> He wore the ordinary seaman's dress, with the stoker's 'screw' on his right arm, and short leggings. Instead of a sailor's cap he had an ordinary grey cap, which with his Naval clothes, looked decidedly incongruous out of doors.[113]

At 11 o'clock the prisoner was brought into court and charged in the name of Hubert Cyril John Mitchell. The *Weekly Dispatch* detected a mood of sympathy for Mitchell because 'it was generally believed he had committed the crime during a seizure of epilepsy'.[114] Presiding on the Bench were Sydney Jolliffe and Albert Johnson.

It was a preliminary hearing to determine whether the prosecution had sufficient evidence to justify committing the accused for trial at the Winchester Assizes. The defence case was not heard at all. The prosecution was led by Mr Wilfrid Rooke-Ley, who was conducting the case on behalf of the Director of Public Prosecutions.

Rooke-Ley opened his address with a bold statement — there was no doubt, he declared, that Mitchell had killed Mrs Treble. He intended to present evidence to the court that proved beyond question that the accused man had fired the fatal shot. However, he respectfully submitted that the prisoner's state of mind at the time of the murder need not concern the Magistrates — that was a question for the doctors to decide after they had examined the man in person and studied all the facts and the depositions in the case. The Chairman of the Magistrates agreed: it would shorten proceedings greatly if they confined themselves simply to the material facts of the case as they related to the question of who fired the shot that killed Mrs Treble.

The impression given was that the prosecution case against Mitchell was so conclusive and so free from taint that the whole drama was nothing more than a formality.

113 *Hampshire Chronicle*, 25 August 1906.
114 *Weekly Dispatch*, 2 September 1906.

Evidence was taken from a small number of witnesses, most of whom had already testified at the inquest. Amelia Treble spoke again of her sister-in-law falling against the walls of the stable; Albert Clarke and William Aldridge (still in his torn trousers, still hobbling) practically repeated their previous testimony word for word.

A new witness was Douglas Fleet Goldsmith. Despite the court's undertaking to confine the proceedings to the actual shooting of Mrs Treble, Goldsmith was encouraged to give a full account of his actions from the moment he spoke to the road mender at Gravel Hill to the victory parade on Winchester Road. It was a boy's own adventure story straight out of the pages of *Chums* magazine featuring dashing 'Heart of Gold' Goldsmith as the plucky hero and Bertie Mitchell as the swarthy, demented arch-villain. At the end of his evidence, Rooke-Ley asked the witness to clarify one crucial point regards the actual shooting of Mrs Treble:

> Rooke-Ley: When you heard a shot fired in Station Road, and you were looking out from Charles Street, did you know that was the shot which struck Mrs Treble?
> Goldsmith: I was told so — a woman.

Here was the prosecution's key witness admitting in court he didn't actually know who shot Mrs Treble. He said he heard a second rifle shot (although no one else heard it, apart from Clarke) which an unidentified person later told him had struck some woman or other. That was it. This was the Crown's 'proof beyond question' that Mitchell had fired the fatal shot.

Police Sergeant Allen and Constable Stockwell followed in the same vein, giving lurid accounts of the chase and capture of Mitchell across the open fields. Henry Birch fidgeted in the dock as he endeavoured to explain how the prisoner had smuggled so much ammunition out of a high-security military firing range.

Inevitably, Dr Cross was summoned to appear as a witness. He recounted his two interviews with the prisoner at Petersfield police station. Again, the court strayed from its remit and invited the doctor to offer an opinion on the prisoner's mental condition. 'In my view,' announced Cross, 'at the time he fired the fatal shot the prisoner was suffering from post-epileptic mania.'

Throughout the proceedings, Mitchell had been given the opportunity to cross-examine witnesses. But of course, he had no legal training — he didn't understand the rules of evidence or the workings of the criminal justice system. And besides, as we have seen, he was not in a position to counter any of the evidence because he was feigning partial amnesia for the crime. All he could do was come out with a vague, general statement, which, if anything, served purely to validate the diagnosis of Dr Cross:

> I never saw the woman. I don't remember anything about the woman, she is a complete stranger to me. I don't remember firing the shot not till they

told me the next morning. I don't know how I got to Petersfield, as I have never been there before in my life.[115]

He was asked if he wanted to call any witnesses. But realistically, who was he going to call? William Tew? 'I have several, sir, but I don't think it is much good calling them now.' He may have been referring to Harry Bentley and sick-bay steward William Windsor (both of whom were in court), who had given evidence at the inquest. 'What do you want to call them for?' asked Jolliffe. At this stage, instead of defending himself against the charge of homicide, Mitchell was still desperately pursuing his 'master plan' — feign memory loss, acquiesce to the 'epileptic mania' diagnosis, get discharged from the Royal Navy, regain his sanity while in hospital, walk away a free man. As Mitchell saw it, Bentley and Windsor might have strengthened the conviction that he was deranged and not responsible for his actions: 'They will show I was weak and wasn't fit-like at the time' is how Mitchell phrased it. But Jolliffe and Rooke-Ley explained to Mitchell that now wasn't the time to go into these matters — the prisoner's health and state of mind would be fully examined at the proper juncture.

Jolliffe had made his mind up.

> It appears from the evidence that Mrs Treble was killed by a shot fired by yourself, and upon that evidence we commit you to take your trial at the next Assizes at Winchester.[116]

Mitchell was removed from Court. Later that afternoon he was escorted to the railway station and placed on the 3.35 train to Portsmouth. A large crowd gathered to watch his departure. In the early evening he was taken by cab to Winchester prison to await trial.

*

So far as the people of Petersfield were concerned, the drama of the 'mad sailor' ended here. Life quickly got back to normal; the murder spot lost its grisly attraction and Margaret Treble's death was soon forgotten. The shattered window panes at the Council offices were replaced.

The *Hampshire Post* reflected on the vagaries of notoriety:

> The sensation caused by the remarkable escapades of the mad sailor in Petersfield a fortnight since has subsided. Animated conversations of the event have ceased, personal experiences and hair-breadth escapes are no longer recounted, and even the tonsorial artist who wields his razor with such marked dexterity has found other topics for discussion.[117]

115 *Hampshire Chronicle*, 25 August 1906.
116 Ibid.
117 *Hampshire Post*, 31 August 1906.

On Monday 27 August there was 13-a-side cricket match on the Heath — Petersfield Tradesmen v. Police. Superintendent King and Sergeant Allen took part, and among the opposition players were Henry Caplen and Albert Clarke. The newspaper proprietor A.W. Childs acted as one of the umpires, while the magistrate Albert Johnson made himself useful by overseeing the luncheon arrangements. It was a light-hearted game, conducted in good spirits, the police ending up the eventual winners by an innings and nineteen runs. However, there was a rather bad-tempered write-up about the game in the *Hampshire Post*, which appeared right next to the paper's report on the Mitchell committal.[118] It was a sad reflection on the newspaper's ethics that a friendly sporting knockabout on the Heath between two amateur teams should provoke so much bitterness, while nothing at all was said about the far greater injustice that had taken place in the Petersfield courtroom the week before.

*

A rather macabre attempt to wrest some commercial leverage from the shooting tragedy came with the printing of a souvenir postcard by Petersfield photographic artist Louis Hayward, who ran a studio from his home at 35 Windsor Road. The photograph shows a bullet and an empty cartridge case allegedly fired by Herbert Mitchell. According to the *Hampshire Post*, the bullet had been retrieved near the railway station, and the case in Stroud.[119] An article in the *Bulletin* of the Petersfield Area Historical Society remarks that

> The production of such a postcard seems bizarre to modern society, but it was during the hey-day of the picture postcard collecting era and, also, no doubt was a best seller to the residents of Petersfield, eager to obtain a souvenir of one of the most sensational occasions the town has ever witnessed.[120]

*

In October, William Tew and his son won a prize each in a handicap tournament at the ninth annual general meeting of the Petersfield Chess Club.[121] Life goes on.

118 Ibid.
119 *Hampshire Post*, 7 September 1906.
120 'Petersfield's Day of Terror — Affair of the Mad Sailor', *Bulletin Petersfield Area Historical Society*, Vol. 5, No. 10 (Autumn 2000), p.6. One of the postcards has survived and is preserved at the Petersfield Museum (ref. PTFPM:2012.601).
121 *Hants and Sussex News*, 10 October 1906.

7

The Trial

At Winchester prison Mitchell came under the care of Dr Thomas Decimus Richards. Born in Redruth, Cornwall in 1857, Richards passed the membership examinations for the Royal College of Surgeons of Edinburgh in 1883. He began his medical career as a general practitioner in Winchester, shortly afterwards becoming medical officer at the prison. He acted also as surgeon for the county police. He was a highly esteemed member of the medical profession at Winchester, and during a career that lasted well over forty years regularly gave evidence at the Assizes and Quarter Sessions.[122]

Dr Richards was actually on leave when Mitchell was admitted to the prison. Assessment of the prisoner therefore had to wait until the doctor's return in early September. He had Mitchell moved to the hospital ward for observation. It seems Mitchell had two 'epileptic fits' during the entire time he was at Winchester from 24 August to 23 November. Dr Richards himself never witnessed the prisoner having a seizure or behaving in a violent manner; his diagnosis of epileptic mania was therefore based completely on reports presented to him second hand by hospital attendants and orderlies. At the committal hearing, the Clerk of the Magistrates had assured Mitchell that 'Everything will be done for you [at Winchester] and the fullest investigation will be made', but in truth only a cursory medico-psychological examination was undertaken at the prison, and no effort was made by Richards or anyone else to determine the genuineness of Mitchell's symptoms of insanity or the state of his mental health.

Apparently, during the first fit the prisoner became irritable and lashed out at one of the prison officers, then fell to the ground in a state of drowsiness; during the second fit he fell to the ground first, got up and became irritable. From this, Richards concluded that the prisoner was of 'unsound mind'. At the forthcoming trial, he would tell the jury that on the afternoon of 17 August, in Petersfield, Mitchell had been unable to distinguish right from wrong, and had not been responsible for his actions.

Of course, Mitchell was still feigning 'fainting fits' at Winchester. His own account of these 'fits' and violent interludes is very different from the official version presented by Richards:

> One of officers in charge of me was always quoting passages of scripture to me night and day. I got tired of it and one night struck him and struggled with him. I fully expected to get punished for this, but instead they said it was a fit and let me alone.[123]

122 'Death of Dr T. D. Richards', *Hampshire Telegraph* 23 May 1930.
123 D/H14/02/2/1/2157 Statement from Herbert C. J. Mitchell to Superintendent Brayn, 7 May 1907.

We have to conclude that Mitchell was happy enough to play along with the doctor's diagnosis of him as an epileptic maniac. After all, he must have known that without an insanity defence he would be executed for the murder of Margaret Treble; it was no doubt the better course of action for him to be considered deranged and then to 'recover' and leave the hospital or the asylum as a free man than to be hung by the neck as a convicted murderer behind the walls at Winchester prison.

*

Epileptic mania was a favourite malady of the Victorian and Edwardian period. The dramatic external symptoms of the 'disease' — the tonic spasms and chronic convulsions, the foaming at the mouth, the falling sickness — were well known and fully documented, if not properly understood, but it was the *masked* form of epilepsy associated with temporary changes in personality causing fits of aggressiveness that principally concerned the men of science. Writing in 1911, W. R. Dalzell identified the problem:

> The difficulty and danger lie rather in the masked forms of epilepsy whose very obscurity constitutes one of the gravest menaces to the unfortunate victim of the disease or to the public at large, who are exposed to the sudden and unprovoked murderous attacks of irresponsible maniacs who may themselves be quite unconscious of the terrible outrages they commit in their frenzied paroxysms of impulsive fury . . . which will probably result in their being brought before a judge and jury to stand their trial on a capital charge.[124]

We have already discussed the case of Lance-Corporal Henry Spurrier, diagnosed as an epileptic maniac, who in 1898 stabbed a comrade to death while recovering from a seizure. Many other important criminal cases from the last quarter of the nineteenth century involved the diagnosis of epilepsy. In 1876 a young man called Frederick Treadaway, who was 'admittedly sane before the act and admittedly sane after committing it', murdered John Collins at Pimlico by shooting him in the face. At his Old Bailey trial it was stated in Treadaway's defence that he was suffering from 'epileptic vertigo' and was therefore unconscious of his actions at the time of the shooting. While Treadaway was found guilty and sentenced to death, the Home Office commuted the sentence on compassionate grounds to penal servitude for life.[125]

That same year, William Drant ran out into the street in Hemingby, Lincolnshire, swinging a wooden fence railing around like a cudgel. He struck police constable Thomas Gell several times on the head, killing him. Like

124 W. R. Dalzell, 'The relation of epilepsy to crime', *Journal of the Royal Institute of Public Health*, Vol. 19, No. 6 (June, 1911), pp.332–333.
125 Old Bailey Proceedings Online (www.oldbaileyonline.org), trial of Frederick Treadaway (t18770205-246).

Treadaway, Drant was sentenced to death for murder. However, the psychiatrist Henry Maudsley wrote to *The Times* about the case, arguing that Drant suffered from 'epileptic mania', a disorder 'well known to have most furious and dangerous consequences', and was therefore not responsible for his actions. Drant was eventually reprieved.

The alienist Dr Lyttleton Forbes Winslow even put forward the view that Jack the Ripper may have been an epileptic:

> I imagined that Jack the Ripper suffered from this malady, and that, during the seizure, he might perform the most extraordinary and most diabolical actions, and upon his return to consciousness would be in perfect ignorance of what had transpired when the attack was on him, and would conduct himself in an ordinary manner before people.[126]

Forbes Winslow also took an interest in the case of Mary Pearcey, claiming her murder of Phoebe and Tiggie Hogg in 1890 occurred while she was under the influence of epileptic mania. Other doctors came to a contrary view, however, and Pearcey was executed at Newgate prison.[127]

*

The Hampshire Assizes and Quarter Sessions were always held in the Great Hall at Winchester Castle. Sir Walter Raleigh was tried there for treason in 1603, and in 1685 it was the scene of the 'Bloody Assizes' at which 'Hanging' Judge Jeffreys presided in the aftermath of the Battle of Sedgemoor. Frederick Baker was convicted at Winchester in December 1867 for the murder of Fanny Adams,[128] and twenty-one years later Robert Husband stood in the dock at the Castle charged with the murder of eight-year-old Percy Knight Searle.[129]

The Winter Assizes for 1906 were opened at the Castle on Wednesday morning, 21 November. His Lordship Mr Justice Kennedy had arrived in the city in the pouring rain just a little before midnight on Tuesday evening. As usual he attended morning service at the Cathedral before being driven to the Castle in the Sheriff's carriage.

The calendar contained the names of forty-three prisoners, among them Arthur Lucas, charged with maliciously setting fire to a dwelling house at Ellingham, and Charles Figes, a fireman, charged with attempting to commit suicide by taking oxalic acid. Also appearing was James Finden, indicted for stealing a box of haddock and ten bloaters worth 5s. But there was only one

126 L. Forbes Winslow, *Recollections of Forty Years* (London: John Ousley Ltd, 1910), p.258.
127 See Sarah Beth Hopton, *Woman at the Devil's Door* (London: Mango Books, 2017). For a twentieth century case involving a failed epilepsy defence for murder, see Kate Clarke's study of the butler Charles Houghton in her compendium *Deadly Service* (London: Mango Books, 2015), pp.117–131.
128 See David Green (ed.), *Trial of Frederick Baker* (London: Mango Books, 2021).
129 See David Green, *The Havant Boy Ripper* (London: Mango Books, 2018).

capital charge — that of Herbert Mitchell, the mad sailor of Petersfield, for the murder of Margaret Treble.

*

The trial of Herbert Cyril John Mitchell took place on Saturday, 24 November. At ten o'clock exactly, the door of the court was flung open and in strode Mr Justice Kennedy, followed by the High Sheriff. Everyone stood up. The Judge thundered across the hall in his crimson robes and freshly powdered wig, and assumed his seat on the Bench.

The Clerk of the Peace ordered the gaolers to fetch the prisoner, and at two minutes past ten Mitchell was ushered into court. Immediately, the charge was read out to him — that on 17 August, in Petersfield, he did wilfully murder Margaret Treble by shooting her with a rifle. In a low, almost inaudible voice, and with head bowed, he pleaded not guilty.

In little more than an hour, the trial would be over.

William Rann Kennedy (1846–1915) was considered 'a careful and conscientious Judge — somewhat slow and laboured both in the formation and the expression of his opinion, but usually sound in his method of reaching conclusions, and accurate in the result.'[130] After an education at Eton and Cambridge, he was called to the Bar at Lincoln's Inn in January 1871. His early legal career was spent at Liverpool, where he concentrated on shipping cases and marine insurance law. He became a barrister in 1882, a QC in 1885, and he was raised to the Bench in 1892. Politically, he was a Liberal, although he failed three times to enter Parliament.[131]

Prosecuting on behalf of the Treasury was the young barrister John Allsebrook Simon. At the start of the year he had been elected Liberal MP for Walthamstow. Ultimately he would go on to attain high office as a politician, being promoted to Attorney-General in 1910 at the age of thirty-seven, and becoming Home Secretary twice, but many commentators felt he was a rather dull, lacklustre performer in court; he lacked flair and warmth, and juries tended to switch off when he started talking.[132]

The defence was represented by Henry Brodrick, who practised mainly on the Western Circuit. It seems he was brought in at the very last moment by the instructing solicitors Godwin & Co of Winchester after their first and second choices of barrister pulled out. Much later in his career, Brodrick would be appointed a Metropolitan police magistrate, making use of his supposed extensive knowledge of the criminal haunts of London: 'No one is more familiar with the underworld life of London than Mr Brodrick', crowed the *Illustrated Police News*.[133]

130 'A scholarly judge', *Evening Mail*, 18 January 1915.
131 See 'The Right Hon. Sir William Rann Kennedy, LL.D, F.B.A', *Journal of the Society of Comparative Legislation*, Vol. 15, No. 2 (1915), pp.66–71.
132 David Dutton has written a biography of him, *Simon: A Political Biography of Sir John Simon* (Aurum Press, 1992).
133 'New London Magistrate', *Illustrated Police News*, 5 April 1928.

Standing in the dock, gripping the rail with both hands, Mitchell seemed 'a forlorn and hapless figure'.[134] He was smartly dressed in a dark reefer jacket over his seaman's uniform, but he looked pale and careworn. The courtroom was half empty. Glancing around, he noticed Lieutenant Herbert occupying a seat just below the dock, and at the back of the room he spotted Mr Harvey from the Admiralty, along with several other naval men he did not recognise. Relatives of Margaret Treble were seated to his right, and on his left were the jury and press benches. And the man at the table in front of him was apparently his defence barrister, although no one had bothered to introduce them. Had Mitchell's wife made the journey from Sydenham to be in court? Was Herbert's mother present, or any of his half-brothers and sisters? We don't know, but it seems almost certain that Mitchell was utterly alone.

Mr Simon opened the prosecution by giving the jury a summary of the facts of the case — he described Mitchell's escape from the firing range at Tipner with a service rifle and ammunition, his journey to Petersfield, his march through the town shooting at people at random, and how he deliberately shot Mrs Treble with murderous intent and killed the poor lady. He spent almost as much time lauding the 'great courage' of Douglas Fleet Goldsmith, who had brought down and disarmed the prisoner despite himself being fired at repeatedly.

> I understand from what Mr Brodrick tells me that these facts are not going to be disputed on the prisoner's part. The defence will be not that the prisoner did not murder Mrs Treble but that he was suffering from an excess of insanity at the time, and I have to say the prosecution shares this view that this man did show all the signs of being under an insane delusion at the time.[135]

Thus, there were two matters the jury needed to consider: first, were they satisfied that Mitchell was guilty of murder, and second, at the time he committed the offence, was he acting under the impulse of an epileptic mania that rendered him not responsible for his actions. The prosecution would adduce sufficient evidence to prove the first matter; the defence would call witnesses to prove the second. In this way, Mr Simon concluded, the proper verdict would be that Mitchell was guilty of murder but insane.

Mitchell may have wondered what was going on. He had pleaded not guilty yet his defence counsel had already spoken with the prosecution and they had agreed among themselves, before the trial even started, that he was guilty.

Mr Simon then proceeded to call witnesses. They were the usual faces giving pretty much the same evidence they had uttered at the inquest and the committal hearing.

Henry Birch was first up, followed by Fleet Goldsmith, who had 'tweaked' his testimony since giving evidence at the committal hearing. Back in August he claimed Mitchell had opened fire on him at the top end of Charles Street,

134 *Hants and Sussex News*, 28 November 1906.
135 Ibid.

and had then fired a second shot that supposedly struck Mrs Treble; now, at the trial, he stated that Mitchell had only *aimed* at him but that all the shots were actually fired in Mrs Treble's direction. This inconsistency wasn't picked up by the prosecution or the defence, despite both counsels having copies of the auctioneer's deposition from the lower court. Fleet Goldsmith was far more interested in spinning an exciting yarn about his pursuit of Mitchell across the fields and the bagging of his prey outside the pub in Stroud.

Amelia Maud Treble gave her evidence, and then PC Stockwell. William Aldridge had also made the trip to Winchester to testify. He limped into court in his dirty, torn trousers, and wobbled a little getting into the witness box. He seemed miffed when the Judge failed to offer him a chair so that he could take the weight off his 'injured' left limb. He showed the Judge the cut in the cloth, and spouted the familiar lies.

The last witness for the prosecution was Dr Robert Cross. The doctor gave evidence of the 'utmost importance': he testified how he had attended Mitchell at the police station to see if his gunshot wounds were serious. The prisoner seemed dazed, he said, and complained of a pain in his head. After speaking to him, Dr Cross formed the opinion that Mitchell was suffering from epileptic mania and didn't know what he was doing at the time he shot Mrs Treble. Brodrick and Mr Justice Kennedy cross-examined the witness, but only in a very cursory way — they ought to have asked Cross what his qualifications were for pronouncing the defendant 'insane'; they ought to have enquired into the extent of the doctor's medical training and clinical experience that enabled him to diagnose 'epileptic mania' so confidently.

His Lordship wanted to know if Mitchell had a visible fit before the mania overcame him, a fit that people ought to have seen. Dr Cross didn't know — he wasn't there — but that didn't stop him from telling the Judge, 'No, my lord, he did not have a visible fit. Sometimes it [the homicidal mania] comes on after a fit, and sometimes it takes the place of a fit altogether.' This was just waffle, an attempt by Cross to cover all bases by describing vague and ill-defined, catch-all symptoms.

Mitchell's statement to the magistrates at the end of the committal hearing was then read out in the Castle: 'I don't remember firing the shot not till they told me the next morning. I don't know how I got to Petersfield, as I have never been there before in my life.' And that concluded the case for the prosecution.

*

It was difficult to differentiate the defence case from the prosecution case because they both assumed Mitchell was guilty and they both assumed he was an epileptic maniac. The one was effectively a continuation of the other. Mr Brodrick called two witnesses — Dr James McGregor from Portsmouth prison and Dr Thomas Richards from Winchester prison. Both men concurred with Dr Cross that Mitchell was a homicidal epileptic maniac, but they disagreed amongst themselves as to the nature of the prisoner's epilepsy. Dr Cross didn't believe Mitchell had had a fit before he attacked Mrs Treble. Dr McGregor thought Mitchell had had a fit seven hours before he attacked Mrs Treble (while he was sitting on the toilet at Tipner). Dr Richards didn't know either way but he felt the prisoner could be dangerous or lucid (or both) before an attack, during it, or after. It was all very confusing. What the doctors could agree on, though, was that none of them had witnessed Mitchell having an epileptic fit, none of them had ever seen Mitchell behave in a violent manner, none of them had any reservations about accepting at face value Mitchell's ramblings concerning his violent past. Yet somehow they had all reached the consensus that Mitchell was a homicidal epileptic maniac who did not know the difference between right and wrong and was not responsible for his actions.

Brodrick felt there was no need for him to present a closing speech to the jury because in his view 'there could not possibly be a clearer case of insanity'. The Judge agreed, and turning to the jury told them that he didn't intend to summarise the evidence either as he would normally do in a trial. 'It was quite clear,' he remarked, 'that the woman did meet her death from a bullet, and there was abundant evidence that this man fired the shot and intended to do so.'

And that was that. All that was left was for the Judge to commend the 'courage and presence of mind' of the glorious Douglas Fleet Goldsmith.

The jury didn't bother retiring to consider their verdict. There was no need. A few nods of the head and it all was agreed: Guilty of wilful murder, but insane. The Judge ordered the prisoner to be detained in a criminal lunatic asylum during His Majesty's pleasure.

Mitchell picked up his cap, turned on his heel, and was bustled out of court by the gaolers.

*

Mitchell felt aggrieved at the way he had been treated by the criminal justice system. He hadn't been given the opportunity to discuss his defence with his barrister; nor had the solicitors appointed to act for him contacted him at any time during the three months leading up to the trial to let him know what was going on. In his statement to the Broadmoor authorities, he complained that

> I had fully made up my mind to tell the truth, but they conducted the trial without speaking to me. It was all over and I was sentenced before I knew where I was. Just as I was about to speak, I was shoved down the stairs.[136]

The verdict of guilty but insane had been available to juries since the passing of the Trial of Lunatics Act in 1883. It was a special verdict that did not represent a conviction on the indictment but was always accompanied by the stipulation that the accused party should be detained 'at His Majesty's pleasure' in a lunatic asylum. There was no right of appeal in such cases.

136 D/H14/02/2/1/2157 Statement from Herbert C. J. Mitchell to Superintendent Brayn, 7 May 1907.

If Mitchell thought he was going to be transferred to Haslar for observation, he was badly mistaken. He was escorted back to Winchester for a few days while the Home Office made arrangements for his admission to a criminal lunatic asylum. The warrant of removal came through quickly,[137] and on Thursday, 29 November 1906, Herbert Mitchell and two warders from Winchester prison travelled by train to the Berkshire station of Wellington College for Crowthorne. Outside there was a carriage waiting to take them up the hillside and along the wooded country roads. In no time at all they reached the red brick buildings of Broadmoor Lunatic Asylum.

137 D/H14/02/2/1/2157 Warrant of removal of a Criminal Lunatic from Prison to Broadmoor, 26 November 1906.

8

'His Majesty's Pleasure Man'

There was a widely-held belief that being committed to Broadmoor was a 'death-in-life' sentence for its inmates. As the *Morning Post* once wrote:

> The inhabitants are separated from their fellows by the double barrier of crime and madness . . . When the gates of the asylum close behind them they are shut off from society for ever. The days will grow to weeks, the weeks to months, the months will add themselves and make years, and they will still remain immured while the world rolls on unheedful of them.[138]

While it is true that the majority of Broadmoor's inhabitants were never set free, every year a number of patients managed to secure their release. The discharge of a patient from Broadmoor rested ultimately with the Home Secretary, who needed to take into account not only the interests of the patient but those of society as a whole.

Mitchell no doubt anticipated that his stay at the asylum would be short and relatively trouble-free. For the past six months he had been feigning mental illness in the hope of obtaining compassionate leave from the Navy; he probably reckoned that all he needed to do now was behave sanely for a while and he would be released. But at Broadmoor patients were never automatically discharged if their lunatic symptoms abated; they were only considered for release after a prolonged period of observation and evidence of stability.

Mitchell never imagined for a moment that he would spend the remainder of his life behind the asylum's sixteen-foot high walls.

*

There were male and female wings at Broadmoor. The male quarters were divided into seven blocks, each housing a different category of patient. Block 4 was the admissions ward. As soon as he arrived, Mitchell was divested of his jacket, cap, and naval uniform, and ordered to bathe in front of the reception officers. He was then given new clothing — grey trousers and a dark blue jacket — and allocated a bed in one of the communal dormitories. He would remain in the admissions block until his mental condition had been assessed. On Monday 3 December he was photographed, head and shoulders, from the front and side.[139]

138 'Criminal Lunatics', *Morning Post*, 27 December 1875.
139 The photographs are available at D/H14/02/2/1/2157. Broadmoor Hospital has a blanket ban on publishing images from patient records, but digital copies of the two admission photographs can be viewed for research or private study purposes on request to the Berkshire Record Office.

Dr Richards was asked to complete a case profile on Mitchell describing his behaviour and mental and physical state of health while he was at Winchester. This profile, called a Schedule A, became the first document in Mitchell's Broadmoor case file (patient number 146,662). Medical officers updated the case files regularly (at least annually) to provide a detailed record of the patient's progress. The following information is taken from Dr Richards's report.[140]

Name:	Herbert Cyril John Mitchell
Age:	24 years
Date of admission:	24 August 1906
Former occupation:	Stoker Royal Navy
From whence brought:	Petersfield Police Court
Married, single, or widower:	Married
How many children:	Two
Age of youngest:	One month
Whether first attack:	Not known
When previous attacks occurred:	Not known
Duration of existing attack:	Before admission into this prison 24 August 1906
State of bodily health:	Good
Whether suicidal or dangerous to others:	Yes, dangerous to others
Supposed cause :	Not known
Whether subject to epilepsy:	Yes
Whether of temperate habits:	No
Degree of Education:	Fair
Religious persuasion:	Wesleyan
Crime:	Wilful murder

140 D/H14/02/2/1/2157 Statement respecting criminal lunatics, 29 November 1906.

When and where tried:	24th November 1906, Winchester Assizes
Verdict of Jury:	Guilty but insane
Sentence:	To be detained during His Majesty's pleasure

Two points are worth noting. First, Mitchell's age is incorrectly given as 24 (he was 23). Second, his youngest child is wrongly recorded as being one month old. We know for certain that Mitchell fathered two children — Albert (born 1902) and Doris (born 1904) — but Mitchell can't possibly have been the father of a third child born in Sydenham in July 1906 because he was still in Dorchester prison when the child was conceived in November 1905.[141]

There are a couple of annotations in a different hand: 'Read and write well' has been appended to Degree of Education, and under Religious persuasion 'Wesleyan' has been crossed out and substituted with 'R. C. 24/11/09'.[142]

Dr Richards's report also contained a description of the patient's 'chief delusions and indications of insanity':

> This man was tried at the Hants Assizes for murder. He [is] a stoker in the navy. Got away from his firing party with a rifle and fourteen rounds of ball cartridge, and went into the town of Petersfield, discharging his rifle at anyone he happened to see, eventually hitting a lady in the thigh causing death from haemorrhage. He is an epileptic. There is a long history of epilepsy and of acts of violence. Since he has been in this prison it has been reported to me by hospital warder Page, H.M. Prison Winchester, that he has had two epileptic fits in this prison and in each case just before the fit he was very violent.[143]

The admissions ward looked out over the Crown estate of Windsor Forest. Across the fields and woodlands you could see Whortleberry Hill and Owlsmoor and the undulating Surrey countryside beyond. Quite possibly the wide open views were intended to be a comfort to newly-admitted patients, encouraging them in the fantasy that they weren't really confined in a criminal lunatic asylum. Even so, Mitchell must have been devastated when an orderly finally took him to his new cell in Block 1. This was one of the 'back blocks' where the

141 Furthermore, there is no mention of a third child in the 1911 census which shows Minnie Mitchell living with Albert and Doris at 60 Dillwyn Road, Lower Sydenham. RG14/2822.
142 In 1909 the Medical Superintendent at Broadmoor had written to the Governor of Dorchester prison enquiring about Mitchell's religious affiliation while he was detained at the prison. The Governor, Ralph Locke, wrote back confirming that Mitchell was a Roman Catholic. D/H14/02/2/1/2157 Letter from Governor of H.M. Prison Dorchester to Medical Superintendent, Broadmoor, regarding prisoner 259 Chas Mitchell, 15 February, 1909.
143 D/H14/02/2/1/2157 Statement respecting criminal lunatics, 29 November 1906.

most dangerous and violent patients were kept. It was rumoured that Jack the Ripper had recently died in Block 1.[144]

> Here are confined the men whose murderous propensities and love of bloodshed seems almost inextinguishable . . . One would hear with less alarm that all the menagerie of Regent's Park was thrown open than that there was even the slightest chance of these men being turned free to prey upon society.[145]

The 'back blocks' were isolated units at the rear of Broadmoor, almost hidden away in the woods that pressed up against their walls. They had their own separate exercise yards enclosed within tall, strong iron railings. The attendants wore special padded jackets, and the patients' food was cut up for them to circumvent the need for sharp cutlery.[146] Lurid newspaper stories exaggerated the horrors:

> Here you observe that the madmen are in separate cells, often with no other furniture than the bed upon the floor. The courteous doctor who takes you round invites you to the little peep-hole to see the wretched creatures inside. If you have not nerves of iron, you will shrink back horrified by the spectacle you see, for there are the most awful types of humanity that the mind can conceive. Observe that fellow there on the floor, his hands are twitching nervously, the only expression in his face is one of wild ferocity, or at other moments one of the dullest of vacuity. But he sees us at the panel; no tiger could spring forward as he springs. The air is rent with a wild, unearthly, inhuman shriek, terrifying to one standing behind the protection of an impassable door.[147]

In part, the opinion of Dr Richards that Mitchell was 'dangerous to others' will have influenced the decision to house him in Block 1, but the attendants and medical officers at Broadmoor were all experienced men and they will have observed their patient carefully and arrived at their own independent assessment. They noticed that he was morose and quick-tempered, quarrelsome and irritable; Block 1 seemed the best place for him, at least to begin with.

*

Mitchell's early years at Broadmoor followed a recurring pattern. He spent protracted periods in Block 1, frequently writing to the chief attendant Charles Coleman or the medical superintendent Dr Richard Brayn petitioning for his transfer to Block 2 or 5 — these were the front wards where trusted and low-risk patients had access to the asylum grounds and could pursue leisure activities and

144 A reference to Thomas Cutbush. See David Bullock, *The Man Who Would be Jack* (Robson Press, 2012) and Cutbush's Broadmoor case file D/H14/02/2/1/1523/1–43.
145 'Broadmoor Criminal Lunatic Asylum', *British Medical Journal* Vol. 1, No. 213 (January 28, 1865), p.96.
146 Ibid.
147 'The Queerest Lunatic Asylum in the World', *Wexford People*, 12 April 1890.

occupy themselves with work. At length he would be moved to one of the privilege blocks, only for him to inevitably start behaving aggressively or belligerently, necessitating his transfer back to Block 1. And the cycle would begin again with more letters of appeal to the asylum authorities.

These outbursts of aggression and ill-temper had nothing to do with Mitchell's supposed epileptic seizures. By nature Mitchell was fractious and easily-riled, and he found it difficult to channel his frustration at being incarcerated. On December 24, 1906, in an attempt to get himself moved to the Infirmary ward (Block 3) over Christmas, he threw one of his pretend 'fainting fits' at locking up time (7.45 p.m.). But the attendant on duty easily saw through Mitchell's ruse — this wasn't the first time a patient had faked epileptic convulsions and mimicked a fainting episode — and he reported the deception to the Chief Attendant.[148] So far as we know, this was the last time Mitchell feigned a fainting fit. Before he arrived at Broadmoor, Mitchell had been diagnosed as a homicidal epileptic maniac by three separate doctors; yet at Broadmoor there are no references to epilepsy in any of his case notes. He suffered no seizures while he was at the asylum, and he experienced no fugues or memory disturbances. The misdiagnosis of epilepsy quietly disappeared from his medical history.

In May the following year, still languishing in Block 1, Mitchell submitted a four-page statement to Dr Brayn. 'I am making this statement,' he wrote, 'to show I am not an epileptic nor insane.'

> I make this statement because I want to get out of this block. I am strong and able to work but I am not allowed to in this block. If you will give me a change to a front block you will find that I shall get on alright and give no trouble to anyone.[149]

This statement represents Mitchell's most detailed account of his actions at Petersfield and his subsequent experiences in prison. We have quoted from it extensively in this book, and the statement is transcribed in full in Appendix I.

Perhaps Mitchell's statement had the desired effect. At any rate, he was transferred to Block 7 later that year.

*

Block 7 was one of the privilege wards. Inmates were allowed into the asylum grounds to work on the estate farms or they helped out in the kitchens and laundry, the flour store or the plumber's shop. They received small payments for their work in the form of credits, which they could redeem on luxuries like tobacco or confectionery. Mitchell had a job as a cleaner and in the summer he also tended the flowerbeds on the terraces.

148 D/H14/02/2/1/2157 Attendant's note: Arthur James (?) to Chief Attendant, 24 December 1906.
149 D/H14/02/2/1/2157 Statement from Herbert C. J. Mitchell to Superintendent Brayn, 7 May 1907.

Patients were encouraged to immerse themselves in the social life of the asylum. There was a cycling club, a brass band, a cricket team and a chess club, as well as an amateur dramatics society. In the early evenings, the inmates retired to the library or the common room. There were occasional fallings out among the patients, and sometimes more serious incidents, but generally the atmosphere was relaxed and convivial. In 1905 the psychiatrist Charles Mercier wrote about life in Broadmoor:

> The homicidal act of an insane person is usually an isolated act, done in a mood of intense exasperation, and not likely to be repeated. Were it otherwise, it is obvious that Broadmoor, in which so many lunatics who have perpetrated homicide find a permanent home, would be a pandemonium of perpetual uproar. It is nothing of the kind. There we see scores of murderers, peacefully and tranquilly pursuing industrial avocations, and giving their custodians no apprehension of renewal of assault.[150]

Mitchell had only been in Block 7 for a few weeks when trouble flared. On 18 January 1908 he had an altercation with another patient, sixty-nine-year-old John Anthony Aldersley.

Aldersley had been committed to Broadmoor in 1903 for setting fire to his apartment in Battersea. As the room filled with flames and smoke, he locked the door and escaped.[151] A former troop sergeant-major in the 5th Lancers, he tended to order his fellow patients around in a brusque, imperious manner. Most of the inmates simply ignored him, but Mitchell couldn't. At 6.15 a.m. on the day in question the two men were washing in the lavatory. Aldersley seems to have spat in Mitchell's ear. They had a few words, and Mitchell struck the other man on the side of the head. Then, when they were going from the dining hall to the dayroom, Mitchell ran up behind Aldersley and pushed him to the floor. An attendant, Percival Holdaway, intervened and Mitchell was secluded at 8.30 a.m.[152]

*

Many patients at Broadmoor suffered from feelings of despair, pessimism, helplessness and self-pity. Mitchell was no exception; he was prone to bouts of 'dismay and melancholy' during which he often turned aggressive and confrontational. In June 1908 Mitchell was particularly restless and discontented. First, he gave up his dusting and window cleaning chores, and then he started issuing verbal threats, telling one of the attendants, Samuel Smith, he would

150 Charles Mercier, *Criminal Responsibility* (Oxford: Clarendon Press, 1905), pp.123-124.
151 'Setting fire to a room', *Eastbourne Chronicle*, 24 January 1903.
152 D/H14/02/2/1/2157 Attendants' notes: Percival Holdaway (?) to Chief Attendant, 18 January 1908; Charles Kellaway (?) to Chief Attendant, 18 January 1908.

'give a little more trouble' in order to get his own way.[153] Later that day he wrote to the superintendent in a more regretful frame of mind:

> Kindly take no notice of my giving up my work. I will carry on with it again if you will allow me, and keep myself in hand more for the future. There is no one more eager to work than myself.[154]

But on July 18, at 10.30 a.m., as the patients were making their way to the airing court for morning exercise, he gave way to his angry impulses and lashed out at Joseph Hutton, striking him without any provocation. Mitchell was immediately transferred back to Block 1.

In a letter to Dr Brayn, undated but clearly composed within a day or two of the assault on Hutton, Mitchell endeavoured to explain his actions:

> You are no doubt surprised at my behaviour in Block 2 and also in Block 7. I should like to tell you the cause of it. Every two years since 1906 either in July or August, I have had strong attacks of melancholia, usually ending in violence of some description but decreasing gradually as I got older. The last attack I cannot account for (August 17th 06) but my opinion is that the state of my health at this time (which was very low) was the cause.
>
> This year 08 if you remember I was very well until July and then I began to worry myself and think over it, dreading a return. I had a very bad time of it. I did not like to tell you the cause but I think it is best that you should know and not misjudge me . . .[155]

Mitchell is describing a summer depression or some sort of seasonal affective disorder brought on by heat or humidity or a surfeit of sunshine. In a later letter to the medical superintendent, dated 22 September 1911, Mitchell specifically mentions his 'head pains' and characterises them as an anniversary reaction to the sunstroke he had in Smyrna in August 1900.[156]

The following summer Mitchell again experienced low spirits coupled with feelings of anger. At his own request he was brought in from the kitchen gardens, complaining that 'he felt he must strike someone'. The deputy superintendent, Dr John Baker, ordered Mitchell's removal to Block 1.[157] As usual, Mitchell's seclusion in Block 1 was followed by an appeal to the superintendent to allow him to return to the front wards:

> I have quite recovered from my recent attack of despondency. I think it was the gloomy weather that was the cause of it . . . Will you kindly send me back to where I came from and my work. You need have no distrust of

153 D/H14/02/2/1/2157 Attendant's note: Samuel Smith to Chief Attendant, 9 June 1908. Smith would later succeed Charles Coleman as Chief Attendant in 1912.
154 D/H14/02/2/1/2157 Letter from Herbert Mitchell to Superintendent Brayn, 9 June 1908.
155 D/H14/02/2/1/2157 Letter from Mitchell to Superintendent Brayn, undated but circa July 1908.
156 D/H14/02/2/1/2157 Letter from Mitchell to Superintendent Baker, 22 September 1911.
157 D/H14/02/2/1/2157 Attendant's note: Frederick William Pulham to chief attendant, 1 June 1909.

me now. I am very glad to think that I am gaining sufficient will-power to control my actions.[158]

Mitchell's warm weather difficulties flared up once more in August 1911. The attendants in Blocks 2 and 3 noted his sullen and sulky moods. He was dismissive of his fellow patients, referring to them as 'dirty and rotten'. He gave up his chores again, and refused food.[159] One of the attendants, Charles Harbour, was tipped off about trouble brewing between Mitchell and another inmate, Harry Bond:

> E. Partridge tells me that during a conversation he had with G. Wells, reference was made to C. Mitchell being upset. Wells remarked that Mitchell had told him that if he met Bond again in the wood shed he would let him know it![160]

Nearly a month later, Mitchell was still volatile. From his cell in Block 1, he demanded a box of playing cards from Dr Alexander Connolly, threatening 'a lot of trouble' if he didn't get them.[161] Yet within a couple of days the worst of the unreasonable excitement had diminished and he was writing apologetic notes to the new medical superintendent, Dr John Baker, who had succeeded Dr Brayn on his retirement in October 1910:

> I am sorry and beg pardon for my impertinence to you the other day. I have had some pains in the head, I always do in August it being the month I had sunstroke. I am better now. I have possessed a good character up to now and will not offend again.[162]

*

Hardly anyone made the effort to visit Mitchell while he was in Broadmoor, just as hardly anyone bothered to turn up for his trial at Winchester. Undoubtedly, the time and expense of travelling to Crowthorne by train from south London will have been an obstacle for some of Mitchell's family and friends. However, we know for certain that Minnie occasionally made the journey to the Berkshire moors to see her husband.

158 D/H14/02/2/1/2157 Letter from Mitchell to Superintendent Brayn, 7 June 1909.
159 D/H14/02/2/1/2157 Attendant's note: Arthur James to Chief Attendant, 29 August 1911.
160 D/H14/02/2/1/2157 Attendant's note: Charles William Harbour to Chief Attendant, 31 August 1911. Ernest Partridge, an inmate at Broadmoor between 1910–1924, was a forty-four-year-old antiques dealer from Raynes Park who murdered his wife by cutting her throat with a razor. He was considered an epileptic maniac (*Westminster Gazette*, 24 May 1910); thirty-five-year-old cellarman George Walter Wells, a patient at Broadmoor between 1910 and 1914, attempted to murder his baby son with a hammer (*Nottingham Evening Post*, 7 April 1910); Harry Bond (55) was a labourer from Oxfordshire who attempted to debauch a girl aged 15 (see *Lincolnshire Chronicle*, 2 May 1902). He was a patient at Broadmoor between 1902 and 1919.
161 D/H14/02/2/1/2157 Attendant's note: Reuben Bourne to Chief Attendant, 20 September 1911.
162 D/H14/02/2/1/2157 Letter from Mitchell to Superintendent Baker, 22 September 1911.

With Herbert away at sea or languishing in prison, and now incarcerated in Broadmoor, life will have been hard for Minnie bringing up two small children on her own. Possibly she was living at Stanton Square in Sydenham throughout 1905 — this was where Minnie's second child, Doris, had been born in 1904. Maybe Minnie was still there in January 1906 when Herbert returned after serving his sentence in Dorchester prison. We don't really know. When he was arrested in Petersfield, he told the police he had relatives residing at 48 Beadnell Road in Forest Hill. This was a double-fronted, five-bedroomed property that had been divided into rooms for letting. It isn't clear who was occupying the property in 1906, although the Weston family had moved in by the time of the 1911 census. Minnie and her children may well have briefly rented a room there when Mitchell joined the Royal Navy for his second term as a stoker.

From time to time, the Mitchell children were 'fostered out' to neighbours or friends. In particular, a Mrs Sarah Bray, who seems to have run an informal 'lying-in' service caring for illegitimate or abandoned children, stepped in to help out. Admittance records for the Lewisham Union workhouse show Doris and Albert Mitchell (aged three and five respectively) entering the workhouse on 11 June 1908; a month later, Albert was discharged into the care of Minnie, now living at 11 Kangley Bridge Road, Lower Sydenham, while Doris was taken to Mrs Bray next door at No. 9.[163] This hand-to-mouth existence is how many working-class families survived in the suburbs of south-east London in the early 1900s.

In 1911 Minnie, Albert and Doris were living at 60 Dillwyn Road in Lower Sydenham. To help make ends meet, Minnie had started taking in foster children of her own — the 1911 census shows eleven-month-old twins, Hilda and Ivy Gaskin, living with the family as nurse children.

Doris enrolled at Sydenham Hill Road school on 6 January 1913.[164] It is highly unlikely she ever met her father; while recognising the risk of patients becoming institutionalised and abandoned by their relatives, the authorities at Broadmoor strongly discouraged visits from children.

*

Mitchell relied less on visits than on correspondence. Patients were allowed to send and receive letters, although all incoming and outgoing communications were censored if they contained false information or were abusive or threatening. For at least a year Mitchell kept up a correspondence with a Mrs Ada Rankin of 4 Hamburgh Place, Hiple Street, in Sydenham: he wrote to her at least once every month, and she replied at the same rate. Nothing is known about Ada or the nature of her relationship with Mitchell beyond the fact that they referred to each other as 'friends'. But in late 1911 or early 1912 there was a falling out of some description: Mitchell stopped writing, Mrs Rankin contacted the Broadmoor authorities to ask why her pen-pal had suddenly gone silent, and Mitchell sent

163 LMA: Lewisham Union workhouse records: Admissions and Discharge Registers: LEBG/198/049.
164 LMA: London School Admissions and Discharges, 1912–1918, LCC/EO/DIV07/SYD2/AD/004.

a letter to Dr Baker complaining about her busybodying. The correspondence lapsed.[165]

*

From 1912 onwards there was a general improvement in Mitchell's condition. He managed to stay out of Block 1 permanently, and he began participating more fully in the social life of the asylum. Inspired by the encouragement of attendant Charles Pike, he took up the violin. He may even have joined the asylum string band, and performed at concerts in the main hall. He also started playing cricket for the Broadmoor First XI, who regularly competed against Sandhurst Royal Military College and other teams from outside. (Perhaps he was reminded of another cricket match at Malta, on a cement pitch covered by cocoa-nut matting, when he was a lad of seventeen on his first voyage abroad.) He hurled himself around the outfield with gusto, on one occasion straining his thigh so badly it needed attention from Dr Alfred Holdaway.[166]

These developments must have given Mitchell hope that he might soon be considered for release. In 1915 three petitions were submitted on his behalf to the Secretary of State for the Home Department. The first was an appeal by Mrs Annie Ansett (*née* Suckling or Suchling), the daughter-in-law of Mitchell's eldest half-sister Elizabeth. The second was a petition sent in by Miss E. Rankcorn, who appears to have been a Mitchell family friend. And the third was a petition from Herbert Mitchell himself. Patients were permitted to write to officials such as the Home Secretary if they had concerns about their detention or their treatment, or they wished to be considered for release. Mitchell probably didn't know it, but the Secretary of State at the time was the Right Honourable Sir John Simon — the same 'dull, lacklustre court performer' who had been in charge of the prosecution at his trial in Winchester in 1906, when he was found guilty of a crime he didn't commit.

The grounds for these petitions will have been based on arguments that Mitchell was now sane or appeared to be sane, that he was exhibiting no signs of mental aberration, that his depressions were giving way to a more equitable and cheerful frame of mind, that he was in greater control of his behaviour, that he had acquired healthy new recreational interests, that all evidence of epileptic mania had long since disappeared (if it ever existed at all), that his general conduct and physical state of health were good, that his capacity for violence (in actuality little more than petty scuffles with fellow patients who irked him) had diminished, that he was obeying the institution's rules.

Individually, each of these factors carried weight, and taken together they constituted a strong case for considering his appeal favourably. In addition, Broadmoor's release policy was far more generous during the First World War than at any time previously in the institution's history, the number of patients

165 D/H14/02/2/1/2157 Letter from Ada Rankin to Superintendent Baker, 10 March 1912; Letter from Mitchell to Superintendent Baker, undated but circa March 1912.
166 D/H14/02/2/1/2157 Note from Dr Alfred George Holdaway to Chief Attendant, 28 March 1913.

being released nearly increasing fourfold. Yet it was almost inevitable that the petitions would fail.

Mitchell's case notes reveal that Superintendent John Baker consistently declined to support Mitchell's petitions for release. While he duly forwarded the petitions to the Home Secretary, they were always accompanied by his recommendation that the patient should remain at Broadmoor. The opinion of the medical superintendent was hallowed and almost unimpeachable: his view of a patient's dangerousness and his risk assessment of the likelihood of a patient re-offending had an undue influence on official decisions over whether a patient should be released.

> This man has a bad history and in view of the nature of his crime his discharge would, in my opinion, be attended with risk of relapse. Altho he has improved mentally during recent years, for some considerable time after admission he was morose, irritable and regarded as dangerous.
>
> He has improved within the past two years but is still unstable and unfit for discharge.[167]

Ernley Blackwell, Legal Assistant Under-Secretary of State at the Home Office, communicated the department's decision on 3 August 1915:

> I am directed to request that you will be good enough to inform Herbert Cyril John Mitchell that his petition of the 28th June has been laid before the Secretary of State, who regrets that he is unable to comply with the prayer thereof.[168]

Mitchell submitted one final petition the following year. By then, Simon had been removed from office and the new incumbent was the Liberal Herbert Samuel. But the result was the same — a damning assessment from Dr Baker and the rejection of the petition by the Secretary of State:

> I have the honour to submit, herewith, a petition from 146,662 Herbert Cyril John Mitchell, praying to be released.
>
> Petitioner although much steadier than he was formerly is unstable in temperament and likely to relapse if exposed to stress or worry.
>
> His statement that he is a bachelor is incorrect. His wife visited him at the Asylum last summer. She informed me that her married life had been unhappy owing to patient's furious outbursts of ill-temper and ill-usage.
>
> I am unable to recommend his application.[169]

*

167 D/H14/02/2/1/2157 Letter from Superintendent Baker to Under Secretary of State at Home Office, 23 July 1915.
168 D/H14/02/2/1/2157 Letter from Ernley Blackwell to Superintendent Baker, 3 August 1915.
169 D/H14/02/2/1/2157 Letter from Superintendent Baker to Under Secretary of State at Home Office, 17 February 1916.

Mitchell fades from view during his final years at Broadmoor. There is a single note in his case book, dated 12 December 1918, recording how he is feeling 'out of sorts and depressed'; he accidentally fell down in his room at night and broke his chamber pot.[170] He comes across as a rather sad, lonely figure, pottering around the wards and half-heartedly tending his flowerbeds. Deep down, he must have had a sense of foreboding about his fate in Broadmoor.

He enjoyed robust physical health until the very end of his life. In July and August 1919 – July and August were always the cruellest months for Mitchell – he developed a persistent cough and began to experience pains in the chest and difficulty breathing. He was transferred to the Infirmary ward. His condition continued to deteriorate, and just after midnight on 2 September, in the presence of Attendant Daniel Hamshire and Chief Attendant Samuel Smith, Herbert Cyril John Mitchell finally died.[171] He was only thirty-five. An inquest was held at the asylum on 5 September before Mr Robert Payne, the Coroner for the Reading District of Berkshire, who recorded a verdict of death from pulmonary phthisis (i.e. tuberculosis).[172] His death from a lung disorder at such an early age may be characteristic of tertiary syphilis.

The formalities were quickly dealt with. The funeral was arranged for Saturday 6 September at 2.30 p.m. in the cemetery adjoining the asylum. A letter was sent to Mrs Mitchell informing her of the death of her husband and notifying her of the date of the funeral.[173]

The cemetery is situated in an area of the forest nearly opposite the entrance to the males' wing. Charles Box describes the lonesome and gloomy place:

> In a hundred yards or so, the resting-place of criminal lunatics is reached, in the midst of fir trees, possessing a silence all its own. Every grave in the shade of these trees contains the remains of a murderer, or a notable felon. The place wears a very grim aspect, and, apart from the slight fencing and cleared space, has an uncared-for look. Owing to the long and rank grass, the visitor might easily imagine himself far, far away from the busy hum of men. Of gravestones, there are none. Each mound is surmounted by an iron cross bearing a number, but neither name nor date lends help to identify the dust below. The funeral inscription is done by book-keeping at Broadmoor; and so the madmen disappear.[174]

There are no records to indicate if anyone at all attended the service besides the gravedigger and the chaplain.

170 D/H14/02/2/1/2157 Attendant's note: James Charles Hull to Chief Attendant, 12 December 1918.
171 D/H14/02/2/1/2157 Case note: William John Ricks, 2 September 1919.
172 D/H14/02/2/1/2157 Notice of inquest verdict on body of Herbert Cyril John Mitchell, 5 September 1919.
173 D/H14/02/2/1/2157 Letter from Superintendent's Clerk to Mrs Mitchell, 2 September 1919.
174 Charles Box, *Elegies and Epitaphs* (Gloucester: H. Osborne, 1892), pp.128–129.

Afterword

Herbert Mitchell's death was mostly overlooked by the newspapers. Even the local press in Hampshire didn't pick up on the story. Bizarrely, one of the few journals to cover the news was the *Larne Times*:

> DEATH OF INSANE MURDERER
>
> The death at the Government Criminal Lunatic Asylum at Broadmoor of Herbert Cyril Mitchell recalls a sensational crime at Petersfield on August 17, 1906.
>
> Deceased, who was then a naval stoker, left a musketry party with which he was firing at Tipnor range, and ran amok through Petersfield, firing at everyone he saw. One of his shots hit a woman, who died soon afterwards.
>
> He was tried at Winchester Assizes, found insane, and sent to Broadmoor.[175]

*

In August 2021 I set out to walk from Tipner firing range to Petersfield, hoping to follow as closely as I could the same fifteen-mile route Herbert Mitchell had taken 118 years earlier. As I journeyed down to the coast by train, I had my first view of the landscape I would traverse on foot later that morning — the allotments and factory yards to the north of the city, the rubbish dumps and recycling plants.

The disused camp at Tipner is fenced off, and security guards patrol the main entrance gates, but if you walk further down the access lane you come to a gap in the hedge that unexpectedly affords a clear view across the range. The high concrete wall still stands at the northern boundary of the ground; there is a badly worn road that leads to derelict buildings at its end, and you can clearly see the raised earthen embankments running across the scrubbed field. I imagined Mitchell in his navy kit mooching around the edges of the camp, waiting for the right moment to abscond.

Today the route from Tipner to Cosham and Waterlooville is mostly urban sprawl. It was only once I got beyond Horndean, where the A3 cuts through the South Downs National Park and the Queen Elizabeth Country Park, that I felt I was crossing landscape that Mitchell might have recognised. The Hogs Lodge Inn (now the Hampshire Hog) is still in business, and I was delighted to come across the Blackman cottage at Gravel Hill where Mitchell had shot into the washing line. I found the place by the roadside where Mitchell had lain down next to the hedge to shoot at the Brickfields cottages.

175 *Larne Times*, 13 September 1919.

Inevitably, landmarks have altered in Petersfield. The Railway Hotel and stable yards were demolished in the mid 1980s to make way for Lavant Court, a forty-two flat retirement complex. However, if you feel the need you can still stand on the spot where Margaret Treble was shot. James Herridge's corner shop at the junction of Charles Street and Station Road is now the Tesco Express. Of course, the level crossing and signal box are still there;[176] since I started work on this book I cannot cross the railway line without thinking of William Aldridge falling off his bicycle. The old cottage hospital in Swan Street where Margaret Treble died was knocked down in 1992.

*

And what happened to the people in our story?

William Tew's cycle business initially thrived. In 1912 he added a second shop at 24 Lavant Street, and in 1914 he went into partnership with his eldest son Frederick. Together they purchased a tyre-repairing business at 4a Station Road, followed two years later by a cycle dealership in Liss. Possibly they expanded too quickly because in 1927 Tew's empire collapsed: crippled by debts and riven with family rivalries, the business went into bankruptcy, the partnership dissolved, and the father moved to Southampton, later to Reading, where he died in 1932.[177] There is nothing to suggest that William Tew ever gave a moment's thought to Margaret Treble, or felt anything approaching remorse for his actions on that fateful afternoon. To be fair to the man, he may not even have realised that it was a bullet from his rifle that entered Mrs Treble's thigh; but if he did, he either didn't care or he dismissed her injury and death as simply collateral damage.

Margaret Treble's husband, Robert, re-married in 1909. He became a farmer with land near Wickham. Sadly, there was unsavoury publicity for the family in 1928 when Robert was convicted of cruelty to animals by allowing two old horses to be worked on the roads in Bere Forest: an RSPCA inspector described the animals as 'bags of bones'.[178] Robert died in 1937 at his farm in Wickham.

Shortly after the First World War, Dr Robert Cross needed a leg amputating and was confined to a wheelchair, although he continued in medical practice. He died in 1932, aged sixty-nine.[179]

Superintendent John King retired in April 1907.

Not much is known about Minnie Mitchell's later years. There are sightings of her at Rowland Grove in Sydenham in 1936 and at Venner Road in Lewisham in 1937, where she is living with her son Albert and Ethel Joan Mitchell (presumably Albert's wife). We are lucky to have a few photographs of Minnie taken in the early 1960s when she would have been in her nineties.

176 The signal box was recently designated a Grade II listed building.
177 'Liss cycle agents ventures', *Hampshire Telegraph,* 15 June 1928.
178 'Horses that were bags of bones', *Hampshire Telegraph,* 3 February 1928.
179 See Bill Gosney, 'Four Doctors named Robert Cross', *Bulletin Petersfield Area Historical Society,* Vol.9, No. 2 (Autumn 2016), pp.9–12.

Doris married William Carpenter, a railway carriage cleaner, in 1927. (Herbert Cyril Mitchell is correctly given as her father on the marriage certificate.) Doris went on to have five children — Francis (b. 1925), Leslie (b. 1927), Edgar (b.1928), Doreen (b. 1933), and Beryl (b. 1936), the eldest of whom was born out of wedlock to a man called Barrett. A photograph of Doris has survived from 1939, the same year she moved down to Plymouth. She died in 1981, aged seventy-six.

*

And finally, we come to the adventure-filled life of Douglas Fleet Goldsmith. There was a whiff of the psychopath about him mixed with the charm of a buccaneer. Instead of pursuing a career as an auctioneer and land valuer, perhaps he ought to have followed in Herbert Mitchell's footsteps and become an apprentice sailor seeking fame and fortune in faraway lands and uncharted seas. He could be polite and mildly amusing when it suited him, but at the same time he terrified people. Throughout his life he oscillated between showy displays of generosity to his business acquaintances and acts of pre-emptive barbarity against complete strangers.

For a while he wallowed in the glory of the Mitchell affair. He married Mary Chalcraft in Liss in 1908, and after a brief honeymoon in Bournemouth the newly-weds moved into their new home at Upper Adhurst, just outside Petersfield. Among the many wedding presents was a hunting crop from Captain William Standish.[180]

Life was good. Their first daughter, Betty, was born the following year. He was elected a county councillor, and he continued to prosper as a farmer and prominent figure in town affairs.

Marrying into the Chalcraft family meant he became owner of Aldersnapp Farm, near Stroud. Goldsmith especially enjoyed the views from the front bedroom windows of the farmhouse, which looked out over the meadows alongside Winchester Road where he had coursed and bagged the mad sailor a couple of years previously.

In May 1924 Goldsmith took part in a six-round charity boxing match against Captain George Darvill, another prominent Petersfield businessman. Although twenty years separated the two men, Goldsmith entered the ring with 'a head of iron grey hair that gave him the appearance of a veteran'. Goldsmith took a punch to the body, followed by a straight left to the jaw; he staggered against the ropes and dropped to the canvas, dazed and groggy. The contest was all over in under thirty seconds.[181] Goldsmith's life and career would shortly suffer a similar knockout blow.

His spectacular fall from grace began on 2 July 1924 at the Petersfield Petty Sessions when he was bound over to keep the peace for 12 months following an extraordinary outburst at a property sale the month before. As auctioneer he

180 'Interesting wedding at Liss', *Hants and Sussex News*, 6 May 1908.
181 'Boxing for charity', *West Sussex Gazette*, 1 May 1924.

refused to accept a bid of £50 for a plot of land, and called the bidder a 'fool'. He then threatened to 'kick him down the stairs' if he did not stay quiet. Goldsmith's reputation as a thug preceded him and the complainant told the Court, 'I thought he was coming along to get hold of me by the throat and throw me downstairs and give me a good hiding'.[182]

On 21 August 1924 he was again brought before the Petersfield Police Court, this time on a more serious charge of common assault.[183] A commercial traveller by the name of Henry Freeman had called at Aldersnapp Farm one morning, but Goldsmith's greeting was far from friendly. He fetched his gun and commenced shooting at the tyres of the visitor's bicycle (just as Mitchell had fired at the soldier's bicycle at Landpits). Then,

> The defendant came after [Freeman] with his hunting crop, bellowed at him like a bull, and threatened to give him 'the damnedst hiding' he had ever had in his life if he did not get off the premises. He struck him on the back with the hunting crop, and called to his man to come and help throw witness in the pond.[184]

All the sordid details of Goldsmith's private life came out in court — the racing horses mutilated in the dark, the paranoid all-night vigils with three dogs and a gun, the boy scout dressed up as a girl and molested in a caravan, the private investigators hired by his wife to watch him night and day. The presiding magistrate was in fact Dr Cross: he sentenced Goldsmith to one month's imprisonment and ordered him to undergo psychiatric examination.[185] In addition, the police applied for forfeiture of the £50 recognisances against Goldsmith and his surety, Mr James Chalcraft, his father-in-law.

Goldsmith was now out of control. On his release from Portsmouth prison, he launched a blizzard of petty and vexatious legal actions. He applied for a summons against the police for robbery with violence, assault and criminal conspiracy, all because they had seized his hunting crop as evidence and refused to give it back immediately.[186]

Events were quickening to their violent conclusion. On the night of 12 December 1924 Goldsmith threatened to shoot and kill a sheriff's bailiff, Thomas Penn, who had entered Aldersnapp Farm on lawful business. He shouted, 'If you are not off my —— premises in five minutes I will get a gun and blow your brains out. Stay out, you dirty dog.' Goldsmith brandished his trademark hunting crop

182 'Threats at a sale', *Portsmouth Evening News*, 3 July 1924.
183 It wasn't the first time he had appeared in court as a defendant. In July 1903 a civil action was taken against him for callously bobby-trapping a woodland track with a spring gun tied to a tripwire ('Spring guns at Horndean', *Hants and Sussex News*, 29 July 1903); in 1908 he wrenched open the locked wicket gate next to the level crossing at Liss because he was late for his train, causing damage to railway property ('How a passenger caught his train', *Hants and Sussex News*, 17 June 1908); in 1913 he was fined for a breach of the Tuberculosis Order of 1913 ('Suspected cow in the market', *Hampshire Telegraph*, 5 September 1913).
184 'Petersfield auctioneer sent to prison', *West Sussex Gazette*, 8 August 1924.
185 Ibid.
186 'Court outburst at Petersfield', *Hampshire Telegraph*, 7 November 1924.

and Penn ran out of the building scared for his life. Minutes later, Goldsmith went out into the gardens with a lantern, hunting for the bailiff and screaming, 'By God, if I get hold of you tonight I will kill you.' By coincidence, that same evening Goldsmith was served divorce papers by his wife and received notice that the Courts had deprived him of custody of his two children — apparently they had been taken to a safe house in Switzerland. In a fury, he drove over to his mother-in-law's house in Liss. He was so enraged at one point he steered the car into a ditch and needed the assistance of two men to extricate it. Arriving at 'The Brows', he demanded to see his wife. When he was told she wasn't there, he shouted, 'I have come for the children, and I mean to have them. Come down and open the door and let me in or I will smash all your b—— windows and burn your house down.' He then proceeded to break all the windows around the house — ten in all. Mrs Chalcraft and other female relatives were petrified and telephoned for the police. At the Police Court on 15 December 1924, Goldsmith was committed for trial at the Winter Assizes for malicious damage.[187] Bail was allowed, but failing to find two sureties of £300 each, the accused was removed to Portsmouth prison.

In February 1925 Goldsmith came before Mr Justice Rowlatt at the Hampshire Assizes. No doubt he remembered well his previous appearance at the Castle nearly twenty years earlier, when he had given evidence against Herbert Mitchell. On that occasion, the judge had praised Goldsmith for his courage and manliness; now, his Lordship had a slightly less exalted opinion of Goldsmith's worth. He was sentenced to nine months' imprisonment in Winchester.[188]

Bullish as ever, Goldsmith took his case to the Court of Criminal Appeal. His plea revolved around his ex-wife: after she walked out, he said, he became 'a little deranged mentally' and seemed to have developed a violent temper. But the appeal judges saw through the sob story. In delivering the judgment of the Court, Mr Justice Shearman said:

> Instead of showing contrition and sorrow prisoner adopted the attitude that he was the victim of a plot. In fact, he was a violent and dangerous man.[189]

The appeal was refused.

Much to the enjoyment of his many enemies in Petersfield, Goldsmith's life continued to implode. In March 1925 he was ousted as a county councillor. In July of the same year he was sued by his partners at the firm of Hall, Pain and Goldsmith – they claimed, not unreasonably, that he had sullied the reputation of the firm; previously the business at Petersfield boasted average annual profits of over £1,000, but in the past year, owing to the Goldsmith crisis, the company was trading at a loss of £269. The partnership was dissolved and then reconstituted

187 'Windows broken and alleged threats at Liss', *Portsmouth Evening News,* 15 December 1924.
188 'Gaol for County Councillor', *The People*, 22 February 1925.
189 *Hampshire Telegraph*, 3 April 1925.

under a different style without Goldsmith's involvement.[190] Finally, and most damagingly, at the end of his prison term Goldsmith was certified a lunatic and transferred from Winchester to the Park Prewett Mental Institution near Basingstoke.

Goldsmith's downfall was complete. He was now a mental patient in his pyjamas, locked away in a Hampshire asylum. During the Second World War Park Prewett was repurposed as a military hospital, becoming internationally renowned as a specialist centre for the treatment of burns and maxillofacial injuries, but when Fleet Goldsmith was there the wards were overcrowded with senile dementia patients and the council had ambitious plans to build cowsheds and pigsties in the asylum grounds.[191]

On the evening of 18 December 1925, Fleet Goldsmith bolted from the asylum and went on the run! He became an escaped lunatic. A madman at large. There was a loophole in the law which meant that if a certified lunatic escaped from an asylum and was not retaken within fourteen days after his escape, he could not be restored to the custody from which he escaped.[192] In other words, if Fleet Goldsmith could evade recapture for a fortnight, he was a free man.

The press loved it. The man who hunted mad sailors was now being hunted himself. The fellow who rejoiced at chasing foxes was now the prey. The newspapers were full of warm extenuations and daredevil accounts of his dash for liberty. They forgot all about his alleged child molestations in a caravan and his threats of murder, the tripwires primed to blow your face off. The old rascal was back. Good old Goldie! Fleet of Foot and Heart of Gold!

In fact, he easily evaded the authorities, and got as far as Dublin, where he was beyond the reach of English law. On his return to London, he sold his story to the *News of the World*. It's such a good yarn we reproduce it in Appendix II.

On Thursday, 7 January 1926, he returned to Petersfield on the 2.25 train from Waterloo. As the carriage clattered over the level crossing he glanced out the window, looking down Station Road at the corner shop and the Railway Hotel stables. Nothing much had changed. Disembarking, he exited the station and walked a hundred yards or so down Lavant Street till he came to the junction with Charles Street. On the corner were the offices and auction rooms of his old firm, now called Hall, Pain and Foster. He will have loitered there a while on the pavement, perhaps ostentatiously lighting his pipe, ensuring he was noticed by his old colleagues working away inside. He wanted them to know the old rogue was back in town. Then he returned to the station forecourt, hailed a taxicab, and drove off to the vicarage in Steep. He had arranged to meet the Press there, so that he could be interviewed.

> Revelling in his hard-won freedom and in the best of spirits, I found Mr. Douglas Fleet Goldsmith, the well-known Hampshire auctioneer, farmer,

190 'Mr Goldsmith sued by partners', *Portsmouth Evening News*, 8 July 1925.
191 'Park Prewett', *Hampshire Advertiser*, 21 February 1925.
192 Lunacy Act (1890), paras 85 & 89.

and former county councillor, whose experiences during the last twelve months have been as sensational as a work of fiction, seated in the vicar's drawing-room in the little village of Steep, near Petersfield, Hants.

'You are a brave man to come and interview a lunatic,' was his greeting, referring smilingly to recent escapades.

Mr. Goldsmith declared that he was never better in his life, and he certainly looked as merry and bright as he was in the old days, when he was popular with all classes and noted throughout the countryside and far beyond the borders of Hampshire for his fearlessness at steeplechasing, in the hunting field, and at feats of horsemanship of any kind. His daring won high praise in the district, and there are many who can still recall the occasion, some years ago, when he went and stalked a mad sailor who had shot and killed a woman in the streets of Petersfield, and effected the man's capture.

After a few minutes' conversation with him I felt assured his sanity was unquestionable.[193]

Later that afternoon, having picked up the keys to Aldersnapp Farm, he walked across the ploughed fields and entered the old farmhouse. He went to the tall looking-glass that hung in the hall and examined himself. A remarkably fit man in his early fifties wearing a grey suit and a bowler hat. He grinned like a maniac. He climbed the staircase that led to the top floor and entered the master bedroom on the right. He stood for a long time at the window, savouring his favourite view over the meadows. He had come home.

*

He enjoyed the life of a gentleman farmer, cultivating his land and walking the dogs. It was the old country pursuits that interested him most — hunting, shooting, and coursing. He built a new hen's hatching house, and oiled his mole traps, but most of his time was spent training and racing horses. In the College Handicap Steeplechase at Windsor in December 1926 he rode his own horse at odds of 100/6 — Escaped Lunatic was its name! He pulled up four fences from home, but it was a gallant effort. As he cantered back to the start in his silver-grey racing colours, he was cheered by the crowd, until he became lost from view in the grey winter haze.[194]

The old anger never totally died out, though — he tried once to summons his mother-in-law, the old hag, for stealing two hounds from Aldersnapp Farm in 1924, but the case was statute barred and the magistrates threw it.[195]

In 1927 he emigrated to Canada, where it seems he enjoyed a retirement of nearly thirty years. He died in 1955 at the age of eighty. As he grew older, perhaps he mellowed a little, although I doubt it. If he ever looked back at his life, there would be few regrets, except for the years wasted in the office and auction

193 'How I escaped from a lunatic asylum', *Reynolds's Newspaper*, 10 January 1926.
194 *Illustrated Sporting and Dramatic News*, 18 December 1926.
195 *Portsmouth Evening News*, 6 May 1926.

rooms. Best of all, he would remember the good times – riding with the pack across Blendworth moor; escaping from the lunatic asylum at night; racing at Windsor; and hunting mad sailors over the fields below Aldersnapp Farm. These were the adventures that gave meaning and purpose to life, that stirred the loins and set the blood aflame.

Appendix I

Herbert Mitchell's Statement

I am making this statement to show I am not an epileptic nor insane.

I was on board HMS Nelson in 1906 undergoing training when I contracted ghonerhea. I did not know what to do with myself it having come to the knowledge of my friends and my shipmates. I could not stand the ridicule. In addition to this I had contracted some debts which I was unable to meet. I thus tried to get sent away from the ship to another ship, but failed. Then I tried to get invalided from the service. I started by feigning fainting fits and attempts at suicide, but nobody said anything about it as I was getting on well at my training. One night I procured a razor and a bottle of black wash and went to the latrine and was sitting on the seat when a shipmate named Bentley came in to the place. He tried to take the things away from me and I struggled with him. Next morning the doctor sent me over to Haslar hospital where I was detained a fortnight and discharged as cured from mental disease. The ghonerhea had also been cured in the meantime and I thought I should be able to carry on alright again so I was sent to do my rifle firing. To reach the range we had a march of about 5 miles and the strain of this must have brought the disease on again.

I did not know what to do. I started feigning fits again when a shipmate in a joke told me it was no good of carrying on that way but I ought to pretend to shoot somebody. I acted on his idea. I procured between 30 to 40 rounds of ammunition and strolled away from the rifle range. I had walked to within a few miles of Petersfield and had spent my money between myself and a respectable tramp on the road. I had several drinks. I came across a party of mounted infantry. One of them gave me some whiskey out of a bottle. I stopped with them about half an hour and they left me. I proceeded on my way and a soldier overtook me on a bicycle and demanded my rifle and ammunition. He presented his carbine at me and said he would shoot but I ascertained that he had no ammunition and I fired over his head to frighten him away. He went.

The firing had attracted the attention of a Mr Goldsmith who was on horseback. He attempted to run over me with his horse. I frightened him away also by firing over his head. I got on a little further when a soldier on a bicycle came up from the opposite direction. I thought it was for me so I broke his wheel. I also continued firing in the air.

I then got to Petersfield where a big crowd was waiting for me. I again continued firing in the air and the people disappeared. I had almost got through the town when Mr Goldsmith appeared and kept on harassing me. There were several police with him. After I was through the town he got a gun and shot me. I had expended all the ammunition then. One of them unfortunately struck the woman which proved fatal. I was not aware of this until next morning when the police told me and charged me with it. How the shot struck her I am unable to say unless it was a ~~richo~~ ricochet. I am a remarkably good shot with a rifle and if that was my intention I could have made every shot tell, but I was only firing over their heads. I cannot tell how it happened. I could not believe it at first and thought they were joking.

I was then taken to Kingston jail and made up my mind to say nothing. I told one person the true facts of the case and he advised me to hold my tongue, telling me I would be alright. I then went to Winchester prison and held my tongue there. I found they had put me down as an epileptic. I was not aware what that meant to me at the time. One of the officers in charge of me there was always quoting passages of scripture to me night and day. I got tired of it and one night struck him and struggled with him. I fully expected to get punished for this, but instead they said it was a fit and let me alone.

At the trial I had fully made up my mind to tell the truth, but they conducted the trial without speaking to me. It was all over and I was sentenced before I knew where I was. Just as I was about to speak, I was shoved down the stairs.

I am completely cured of my last disease and got over my last despondency. I promise that whilst I am here I will carry on perfectly well.

I make this statement because I want to get out of this block. I am strong and able to work but I am not allowed to in this block. If you will give me a change to a front block you will find that I shall ~~be~~ get on alright and give no trouble to anyone.

I remain, yours respectfully

HCJ Mitchell.[196]

196 D/H14/02/2/1/2157 Statement from Herbert C. J. Mitchell to Superintendent Brayn, dated 7 May 1907. Minor punctuation and spelling mistakes have been corrected.

Appendix II

How I Escaped from a Lunatic Asylum

The hunt for Mr Douglas Fleet Goldsmith, who escaped from a lunatic asylum, is ended. The statutory 14 days, during which a person certified as a lunatic may be reclaimed, have elapsed.

Goldsmith, a former member of the Hampshire County Council, and a partner in a firm of auctioneers, was sent to the asylum on being certified at the conclusion of a nine months' term of imprisonment imposed on him by Mr. Justice Rowlatt at Winchester Assizes about 12 months ago.

He made his dash for liberty on the Friday before Christmas, while a concert was in progress in the institution.

When the inmates were being moved from one hall to another he disappeared.

Mr. Goldsmith tells the story of his escape to the 'News of the World.' Upon his release from prison he was conveyed, he explains, to Park Prewett Lunatic Asylum under an order of the Home Secretary. From the first days of his confinement in the institution he determined to bolt at the first opportunity.

The Prize in View

'The prize, by winning through,' as he puts it, 'was to remain at large 14 days, and prove that I was capable of taking care of myself. I laid my plans absolutely unassisted by anyone. I wanted to win off my own bat by my own brains and muscle.

'I thought of trying to escape from the asylum as soon as I got there, but I really could not have done it when I came out of prison, for I was not fit. They treated me very well in the asylum, however, and I carefully trained all through the month. I did a lot of skipping, not, of course with a rope, as they might have thought I wanted to hang myself. I waited until the month was up to see if they would let me out, but when I found there was nothing doing I made my bolt.'

He explained that the patients were allowed to have money to buy extras, but it was retained and doled out as the patients wanted it. Having received a cheque from a relative for £5, he secreted it in his pyjamas at night, and this he was able to get cashed as soon as he got to Newbury.

'Although 50 years of age, I undertook to make a bolt for it in the pitch darkness at 8 p.m. on the Friday, exactly a week before Christmas. I aimed at covering 25 miles over a country of which I had only a most superficial knowledge. North of Basingstoke, to the sea, I knew like a book, and there lay my home and friends. I knew, however, every road would be watched, every police station 'phoned, and, even with my intimate knowledge of this part of Hampshire, capture would follow, even if I reached my father's house, or those of several friends with whom I had been in touch. My plan was to take the most unlikely direction possible. It was for this reason I decided on Newbury. Can anyone wonder that, when we were allowed to go over from Villa Five, where 40 of us lived, to another in Park Prewett, for a concert, that my heart beat with anticipation of the effort of my life?'

The Escape

After consideration, Mr. Goldsmith says he decided to postpone his attempt until the concert was over. 'As we came out in the darkness I threw my overcoat over the shoulders of the patient who was walking alongside me, and shouting to him, "So long, old boy," made my dash for liberty. We had just been shown at a concert a picture of Felix, the Cat who keeps on walking, and I thought to myself that in a quarter of an hour I would be walking too.

'Despite the intense darkness I started on the 25-mile journey at a 100 yards pace. I ran straight down a level road, which took a right-angled turn after going 200 yards. But, if one went straight on, there was no fence, only a 12ft drop down a bank into a ploughed field. I decided to risk the jump, thinking that my pursuers would stand an equal risk with me; whereas they had far less at stake. The bank was reached, and I, travelling at top speed, simply trod on nothing and rolled head over heels, arriving at the bottom shaken, but quite all right. My hunting and steeplechase experiences had stood me in good stead, for I knew how to fall. I was going again in leas than two seconds, only to come a cropper 200 yards further on — over wire, I fancy.

'This fall, being unexpected, winded me, cut my knee, and shook me up considerably. At first I could hear the shouts and whistles of the guards hunting for me. I knew I was only 50 yards from cover — a belt of very thick fir trees — and so I got up and struggled on, and to my joy reached the trees. Another wire fence had to be negotiated, but, on listening, I could hear my guards going away to the left. As soon as I was in the plantation I stopped and somewhat recovered my wind, and then found that my knee, although cut, was not otherwise damaged. So I crept quietly down the plantation at right angles into and across the public road and over another hedge with wire.

The Open Road

'Then I was clear of the Asylum grounds . . . Except for the second fall, everything had worked out according to plan. Further, I could now find my second wind coming back, and away I jogged, avoiding all roads, as I had heard that motor-scouts would be out to scour the roads. After travelling well for about an hour I struck a grassy lane, which I thought ran straight towards Kingsclere. On reaching the end I risked asking a man with a bicycle for a match. No matches are allowed in the Asylum, but I had several packets of cigarettes. I procured a light, and, what was of equal importance, valuable information. I was on the outskirts of Oakley Village — alas! sadly out of line for Kingsclere . . . I altered my direction, and travelled for another hour with the wind at my back. The next cyclist I met also gave me a light and took a cigarette, and I, in an absent-minded way, put his matches in my pocket and set sail again.

Matches 'Worth Untold Gold'

'That box of matches was worth untold gold to me, for I could now look at direction posts. This I quickly did at the next cross roads, and found I was about a mile from Overton. The pleasing intelligence that I was only six miles from Kingsclere bucked me up no end, so much so, in fact, that as the match flickered out I stepped down off a heap of stones onto nothing but thin air, with the result that for the third time that memorable evening I had a fall, again cutting the same knee. However, I picked myself up and set going in earnest. I now decided it was safe to keep to the road and not take any further notice of cars or strange lights.

'It was darker than ever, so dark that I frequently found myself on the grassy side of the road instead of on the metalled path. Another three miles were knocked off. I had now reached the railway by a subway. Nature, however, began to assert herself. I was reeling like a drunken man, and this, I realised, would never do. If I met a policeman and couldn't walk straight inquiries would follow. I spotted a hayrick close by, so in I crept and pulled out a packet of chocolate, of which I ate several bars. Then it came on to rain. I pulled out some of the hay and squeezed in as far as I could. I tried to put in an hour's sleep. This, however, was out of the question. My legs ached, and I felt myself getting stiffer and colder every minute. I was becoming as stiff as a hare. So up on my legs again was the order of the day, and on I went.

A Touch of the Staggers

'Highclere was reached as the clock struck one. Not a living soul about. I took my first drink very sparingly out of the stream, using my hands as a cup. I now made my final effort for Newbury. I knew the road, and as my last match had been used it did not worry me, except that I could have done with another cigarette. Once an aeroplane with full lights flew over my head — it was enough to put the wind up anyone. On reflection I came to the conclusion that the plane was simply a night flyer, but I was not taking any chances at all, and I got under a yew tree quickly and stayed there till the plane was out of sight. Half-way to Newbury I again got a touch of 'staggers' and crept into a cart shed, got into a wagon, and once again took a breather. It was something more than a 20-round contest. I ached all over, and after 20 minutes' rest and more chocolate, I again crawled into the road. By this time I had developed a regular tramp's shuffle. My feet were so tender I could scarcely bear to put them down . . .

'I espied a sergeant of police and a constable walking up the street. I did not wait to be questioned, but explained my plight, and, in reply to inquiries, said truthfully that I had come from Kingsclere on foot, as I was unable to get a bed there. For two hours the cheery sergeant and I talked racing, and at 6.30 I was turned out to find my friend. After much inquiry, he came down, looking more than surprised to see me. His surprise was in no way modified when I informed him I was an escaped criminal lunatic, badly wanted by the police under a special Home Office order.

Smooth Passage to Dublin

'However, ___ was a white man, and I was quickly in the bathroom, after which I had bacon and eggs, until I felt convalescent. He was pessimistic as to my ultimate escape, but I, under the influence of bath and breakfast, was still an optimist. I quickly took the train to Bristol, and there fell in with friends. After consultation, I decided that Old Ireland was a healthy spot. Reinforced with funds – my original fiver had shrunk – I took the 11.50 train for Holyhead, travelling via Crewe and Chester, which I reached at 6.30 next morning. The next morning I bought a fresh outfit, caught the mid-day boat across to Dublin, had a smooth passage, and landed in Dublin, where I stayed for the necessary period before coming back to England.'

The Irish people, he said, were extremely kind to him, and he had a good time there, attending the Leopardstown Steeplechases, riding in Phoenix Park, and hunting with a well-known pack of stag hounds. When it was safe for him to leave Dublin he decided to return to his home at Steep, and came back first to London, where he spent three days.

'Now I am bent on taking up the threads of my life in the neighbourhood where they were broken just about a year ago,' said Mr. Goldsmith, in conclusion, adding that it was good to know that the asylum authorities could not again reclaim him.[197]

197 Amalgamated from the *Hampshire Telegraph*, 8 January 1926 and *Reynolds's Newspaper*, 10 January 1926.

Select Bibliography

Books

Box, Charles, *Elegies and Epitaphs* (Gloucester: H. Osborne, 1892)
Bullock, David, *The Man Who Would be Jack* (Robson Press, 2012)
Chadwick, F. E. et al., *Ocean Steamships* (New York: Charles Scribner's Sons, 1891)
Clarke, Kate, *Deadly Service* (Mango Books, 2015)
Dutton, David, *Simon: A Political Biography of Sir John Simon* (Aurum Press, 1992)
Farnham, Des and Derek Dine, *Petersfield Seen and Remembered* (Hants County Library, 1982)
Green, David, *The Havant Boy Ripper* (Mango Books, 2018)
—— (ed.), *Trial of Frederick Baker* (Mango Books, 2021)
H.M.S.O., *The Musketry Regulations* (London, 1905)
Hopton, Sarah Beth, *Woman at the Devil's Door* (Mango Books, 2017)
Jeffery, David, *Postwar Petersfield* (History Press, 2006)
—— , *Petersfield Through Time* (Amberley Publishing, 2013)
Jones, Spencer, *From Boer War to World War: Tactical Reform in the British Army 1902–1914* (University of Oklahoma Press, 2012)
Machray, Robert, *The Night Side of London* (Philadelphia: J.B. Lippincott Company, 1902)
Margaret, Patricia, *No Wonder I Like Butterflies: A Life of Travel* (Matador, 2013)
Mercier, Charles, *Criminal Responsibility* (Oxford: Clarendon Press, 1905)
Spores, J. C., *Running Amok: An Historical Inquiry* (Athens, OH, 1988)
Standfield, F. G., *A History of East Meon* (Chichester: Phillimore & Co. Ltd, 1984)
Syms, Diana, *Policing Petersfield 1840–2016* (Petersfield Museum, 2019)
Winslow, L. Forbes, *Recollections of Forty Years* (London: John Ousley Ltd, 1910)
Wood, Evelyn, *From Midshipman to Field Marshal* (New York: E.P. Dutton & Co., 1906)

Newspaper and Periodical Sources

Brighton Guardian
British Medical Journal
Bulletin Petersfield Area Historical Society
Cambridge Daily News
Chums
Eastbourne Chronicle
Evening Mail
Hampshire Advertiser
Hampshire Chronicle
Hampshire Post
Hampshire Telegraph
Hants and Sussex News
Herts & Cambs Reporter
Kilburn Times
Medical Journal of Australia

Mid Sussex Times
Illustrated Police News
Illustrated Sporting and Dramatic News
Journal of Mental Science
Journal of the Royal Institute of Public Health
Journal of the Society of Comparative Legislation
Kentish Mercury
Larne Times
Lincolnshire Chronicle
Morning Post
Nottingham Evening Post
The People
Petersfield Papers
Portsmouth Evening News
Reynolds's Newspaper
Salisbury Times
Salisbury and Winchester Journal
Weekly Dispatch
Westminster Gazette
West Sussex Gazette
Wexford People

Public Records Office, Kew

ADM 188/497/305021 — Admiralty: Royal Navy
ADM 188/506/309961 — Admiralty: Royal Navy
ADM 194/185 – Admiralty: Courts Martial Registers Vol. VI 1901 Jan 01 – 1910 Dec 31

Berkshire Record Office

D/H14/02/2/1/1523 (Thomas Cutbush: patient case file)
D/H14/02/2/1/2157 (Herbert Mitchell: patient case file)

Hampshire Record Office

58M99/18 (F.G. Standfield's notes on murder of Margaret Treble)

London Metropolitan Archives

Lewisham Workhouse Admissions and Discharge Registers: LEBG/198/049
London School Admissions and Discharges, 1912-1918, LCC/EO/DIV07/SYD2/AD/004

Petersfield Museum

Herbert Mitchell archive — PTFPM: 2012.601

Acknowledgements

I am very grateful to Judy Gibbons and her daughter Hannah Chandler for help with my research into Herbert Mitchell's marriage and family background. Judy is Herbert's great-granddaughter. They provided me with numerous documents to do with Herbert and Minnie Mitchell's life in Sydenham, as well as rare photographs of Minnie and her daughter Doris. I have welcomed their enthusiastic support for this book.

I would like to acknowledge the cooperation and kind attention of staff at the Berkshire Record Office. In particular, I wish to express my thanks to Ruth King, Archives Assistant. My thanks to the Berkshire Record Office/West London Mental Health NHS Trust for permission to quote from documents in Herbert Mitchell's patient file.

Thanks are also due to the following institutions for valuable assistance: Hampshire Record Office, Portsmouth History Centre, and Petersfield Library. Curator Sophie Yaniw and her staff at the Petersfield Museum were very helpful in facilitating my research and sharing with me the museum's collection of items associated with the Mitchell story.

I am grateful to Mark Ripper for sourcing material for me from the British Library and the National Archives. Bill Citrine kindly worked on the maps and the cover design for me; he has done an excellent job.

For permission to reproduce photographic images and quotations I extend my thanks to: the Francis Frith Collection; Petersfield Museum Limited; Ryan Stevens, the Skate Guard blog and The Jepson-Turner Family Collection for permission to quote from Belita Jepson-Turner's autobiography; Wilson Hill, estate agents, for the photograph of Bottom Cottage, Gravel Hill; Tim Coel and Hülle Architecture and Design for the murder location today photograph.

For reading the first draft of this book, and for much useful advice and encouragement along the way, I extend my thanks to Kate Clarke.

I am much indebted to Helena Wojtczak for allowing me to publish this book through her imprint the Hastings Press, and for her considerable help with the design and production of this book. I appreciate Helena taking time out from her own writing projects to assist me with mine.

Index

A1, HMS (submarine), 39
Adams, Fanny, 71
Adams, Richard, *Watership Down*, 10n16
Aldersley, John Anthony, 82
Aldersnapp Farm, near Stroud, 91, 92–3, 95
Aldridge, William: background and character, 23; falls off bicycle, 23; hides in dairy yard, 24; concocts story, 24; evidence at inquest, 24–5, 36, 40; evidence at committal hearing, 65; testifies at trial, 74
Allen, Sergeant Joseph: confronts Mitchell at Forebridge, 14, 41; heads up Lavant Street, 32; questions and charges Mitchell, 38–9; evidence at committal hearing, 38–9, 65; evidence at inquest, 31, 41; cricket match, 67
amnesia, feigned, 37–8, 39, 42–3, 61, 63, 65
amok, 56–7, 59–60 & n107; *see also* 'rampage violence'
Ansett, Annie, 86
Ansett, Elizabeth (*née* Mitchell) (Herbert's half-sister), 50, 52
Ansett, George, 52

Baker, Frederick, 71
Baker, Dr John, 83, 84, 86, 87
ballistics, forensic, 35–6
Beadnell Road (No. 48), Forest Hill, 85
Bedales school, 31n52
Bentley, Harry: mock fight with Mitchell, 44–5, 58; evidence at inquest, 45; at committal hearing, 66
bicycle battalions, 32
Birch, Henry: at Tipner firing range, 4, 6, 61; searches for Mitchell, 4–5; evidence at inquest, 5, 44; evidence at committal hearing, 65; testifies at trial, 73
Blackman, Allan, 10
Blackman, Susan, 10, 11, 21, 22
Blackwell, Ernley, 87
'Bloody Assizes' (1685), 71
Boer War (1899–1902), 4
Bond, Harry, 84 & n160
Borough Brewery, Petersfield, 29 & n47
Boscombe beach: drowning accident (1893), 23
Bottom Cottage, Gravel Hill, 10, 89
Box, Charles, *Elegies and Epitaphs*, 88
boy signallers, 51
Bray, Sarah, 85
Brayn, Dr Richard, 80, 81, 83, 84
Brickfields cottages, Petersfield, 11, 12, 13 & n24
British Army: training methods and reform, 4; Volunteer movement, 32
British Expeditionary Force, 4
British Medical Journal, 14n27, 80
Broadbent, William, 42
Broadmoor, 76–88; admissions ward, 77, 79; case files, 78–9; cemetery, 88; discharge process, 77, 87; inmates' employment, 81; letter writing, 85; location, 76, 79; management of dangerous and violent patients, 79–80; photographs of patients, 77 & n139; recreational activities, 80, 82, 86; release policy during WWI, 86–7; staff, 80, 83n153, 84; visits from children, 85
Brodrick, Henry, 72, 74, 75
Browndown Camp, near Gosport, 46
Brows, The (house), Liss, 93
bullet, 5n7, 35–6, 67
Bulletin Petersfield Area Historical Society, 67
Burbidge, Joseph (alias of Herbert Mitchell), 4n6, 57
Burgess, Guy, 47n75
Buriton Manor Estate, 10
Burley, Percy, 41 & n64, 43, 45
Butser Hill, 9

Caplen, Henry, 18 & n36, 67
Carpenter, William, 91
Causeway, The, Petersfield, 13 & n24, 31
Chalcraft, James, 92
Chalcraft, Mary *see* Goldsmith, Mary
Chalcraft, Mrs Mary, 93, 95
Chapel Street, Petersfield, 15, 29
Charles Street, Petersfield, 15–16, 25, 26, 29, 32
chess, 32 & n53, 67
Childs, Arthur, 14, 39, 67
Chums (boys' magazine), 54n92
Clarke, Albert: tried for manslaughter as boy, 26–7; leaves Steep, 27; employed at Railway Hotel stables, 16, 27; rushes to help Margaret Treble, 17; observes Mitchell, 17; eyewitness account of shooting, 27–8; evidence at inquest, 27, 36, 40; evidence at committal hearing, 65; cricket match, 67
Clarke, William, 27
Coach and Horses (public house), Gravel Hill, 9, 10, 11, 21
Coffee Tavern, Petersfield, 16
Coleman, Charles, 80, 83n153
Collins, John, 70
committal hearing, Petersfield magistrates' court, 12, 26, 27, 38–9, 63–6
Connolly, Dr Alexander, 84
Cook, Albert, 11 & n19
Coombs, Thomas, 49
coroner's court, Petersfield, 38

Cosham, 7, 8, 89
Cottage Hospital, Petersfield *see* Petersfield Cottage Hospital
Court of Criminal Appeal, 93
Cowplain, 8
Cox & Duffin (motor garage), Sydenham, 56 & n98, 57
cricket, 51 & n84, 67, 86
Cross, Dr Robert George: background and character, 36–7; inexperience and poor judgment, 42 & n66, 43, 46, 74; Dragon Street surgery, 14; tends Mrs Treble, 35; wound theory, 35, 40, 46; uninterested in performing autopsy, 35; tends Mitchell's injuries, 37, 41; interviews Mitchell, 37–8, 39, 43; misdiagnoses epileptic mania, 42–3, 55–6, 58, 65, 74–5; evidence at inquest, 38, 39–40, 41, 42–3, 51–2, 55–6; evidence at committal hearing, 65; testifies at trial, 74–5; sentences Goldsmith, 92; later life and death, 90
Cutbush, Thomas, 80n144

Dalzell, W. R.: on masked epilepsy, 70
Darvill, Captain George, 91
de Robeck, Captain John, 51 & n84
Dillwyn Road (No. 60), Lower Sydenham, 79n141, 85
Dolphin Hotel, Petersfield, 14 & n28, 19n38
Dorchester prison, 56, 79 & n142
Dragon Street, Petersfield, 14, 31
Drant, William, 70–1
Dryad, HMS, 51n84
Dublin, 94, 102

Edgware Road: *amok* incident (March 1906), 57
Enves, Ann, 14
epileptic mania: classification, 42; external symptoms, 70; masked form, 70; Mitchell misdiagnosed, 42–3, 55–6, 58–9, 61, 63, 65, 69–70, 74–5, 81; and relation to homicide, 42, 46, 70–1 & n127
Etherington, Alfred, 12 & n22

Fareham County Lunatic Asylum, 46
Fenn, Edward, 19 & n38, 39
Figes, Charles, 71
Finden, James, 71
Firearms Act (1920), 47n74
Forebridge, Petersfield, 13–14, 31, 41
forensic ballistics, 35–6
Forest of Bere, 7, 90
Fort Regent, St Helier, 52
Fox, Mr (Petersfield hairdresser), 17–18
Freeman, Harry, 92
Freemasons: lodge in Petersfield, 36 & n54
fugue state, 42 & n67, 61

Gander's meat and poultry shop, Dragon Street, 14
Gard, Joseph, 15
Garlogs (manor house), Nether Wallop, 49–50 & n82
Gaskin, Hilda and Ivy, 85
Gell, PC Thomas, 70
George Inn, Portsdown Hill, 7
Gibraltar, 51, 56
Glengarry cap, 25
Goble, Edgar (coroner): background, 39 & n62; William Mellersh inquest, 26–7; Percy Searle inquest, 39n62; James Whatmore inquest, 46; Margaret Treble inquest (*see* inquest on Margaret Treble); censures Goldsmith, 41, 47
Goble, William, 16, 31
Godwin & Co (Winchester solicitors), 72, 75
Goldsmith, Betty, 91
Goldsmith, Douglas Fleet: auctioneer and land valuer, 11; character, 11, 91; member of Petersfield masonic lodge, 36n54; early criminal history, 92n183; at Gravel Hill, 11; accosts Mitchell at Landpits, 11–12; alerts town police, 13; shadows Mitchell, 13–14, 15; at murder location, 15–16; supposed target of Mitchell, 25, 26, 27; eyewitness account of shooting, 26, 27; obtains rifle, 18, 31; would-be big game hunter, 18; stalks and brings down Mitchell, 18; as hero of the hour, 19; offers tours of murder site, 21; stays away from inquest, 26, 41; censured by coroner, 41, 47; evidence at committal hearing, 12, 26, 27, 65; lauded at Mitchell's trial, 73, 75; testifies at trial, 73–4; marriage and first child, 91; becomes owner of Aldersnapp Farm, 91; charity boxing match, 91; spectacular fall from grace, 91–4; sordid private life, 92; imprisoned for common assault, 92; threatens to kill bailiff, 92–3; served divorce papers, 93; terrorises mother-in-law, 93; imprisoned for second time, 93; loses appeal, 93; sued by partners at Hall, Pain and Goldsmith, 93–4; certified a lunatic, 94; at Park Prewett Mental Institution, 94, 99–100; escapes from asylum, 94, 99–102; sells story to *News of the World*, 94; returns to Petersfield, 94; interviewed by press, 94–5; back at Aldersnapp Farm, 95; races at Windsor, 95; failed bid to summons mother-in-law, 95; retirement in Canada, 95–6; death, 95; life's adventures, 96
Goldsmith, Mary (*née* Chalcraft), 91, 93
Grange farmhouse, Petersfield, 14
Grateley railway station, 49
Gravel Hill, near Clanfield, 9, 10, 11, 21, 89
Green Posts Inn, London Road, 5
'guilty but insane' verdict, 46, 73, 75

Hall, Pain and Goldsmith (auctioneers and estate agents), Petersfield, 11, 21, 93–4
Hampshire Advertiser, 30n49
Hampshire Chronicle: on Brickfields cottage incident, 13; on Gard incident, 15; interviews witnesses, 28, 29–30; on Captain Tew, 32, 33; misrepresents George Wilson, 42n65; reports Treble inquest, 56; describes Mitchell at police court, 64; reports committal hearing, 65–6
Hampshire Post, 8, 14, 22, 66, 67
Hampshire Regiment, 3rd (Volunteer) Battalion, 18n36, 32
Hamshire, Daniel, 88
Hannibal, HMS, 55–6
Hants and Sussex News, 21, 47–8
Harbour, Charles, 84
Harrow (public house), Steep, 27
Harvey, E.J., 63, 73
Haslar military hospital, Gosport, 42n65, 43, 45, 58, 59
Hayward, Louis, 67
Heath Road Council offices, Petersfield, 14, 22, 66
Herbert, Lieutenant (of HMS *Nelson*), 73
Herridge, James, 17, 28–9
Herridge's corner shop, Charles Street, 17, 21, 28–9, 30, 90
High Street, Petersfield, 14–15 & n28, 16, 18
Hill, Charles, 15–16 & n32, 28, 32n53
Hilsea, 5, 8
Hobbs, William, 15
Hogg, Phoebe and Tiggie, 71
Hogs Lodge Inn, near Clanfield, 9, 89
Holdaway, Dr Alfred, 86
Holdaway, Percival, 82
Horndean, 7, 8, 89
horse-racing, 95
Houghton, Charles, 71n127
Husband, Robert, 27n43, 71
Hussey, Harry, 23
Hutton, Joseph, 83
Hylton Road, Petersfield, 14

Illustrated Police News, 72
Indian Army: *amok* attacks, 60
inquest on Margaret Treble: Mitchell declines to attend, 39, 40; public interest, 40; viewing of body, 39; evidence presented, 5, 24–5, 27, 31, 36, 38, 39–45, 51–2, 55–6; biased, 40, 45; turns into farce and disgrace, 43, 45; summing up, 30, 45–7; verdict, 47

Jack the Ripper, 71, 80 & n144
Jacobs and Hunt (estate agents), Petersfield, 11n18
Jeffreys, Judge, 71
Jepson-Turner, Belita, 49–50
Jepson-Turner, William, 49–50 & n82
Johnson, Albert, 64, 67
Johnson, Stanley, 15
Jolliffe, Sydney Hylton, 38, 64, 66
Jolly Sailor (public house), Petersfield, 13 & n26
Jubilee celebrations (1887), 50–1

Kangley Bridge Road (No. 11), Lower Sydenham, 85
Kennedy, William Rann (Mr Justice), 71, 72, 74, 75
King, Superintendent John: warned of Mitchell's approach, 13; commands counterattack, 14–15; heads up Lavant Street, 32; at inquest, 36; applies for remand, 39; at Margaret Treble's funeral, 48; cricket match, 67; retirement, 90
Kingston prison, Portsmouth, 39, 63, 92, 93
Kitchener, Lord, 60
Knight, Ben, 13 & n25

Landpits, near Petersfield, 11–12
Larne Times, 89
Lavant Court retirement homes, Petersfield, 90
Lavant Street, Petersfield, 15, 16 & n33, 32, 90, 94
Lee-Metford rifle, 5n7, 14n27, 35–6, 40
Lees hairdressing salon, Petersfield, 17n35
Leonine, Arthur, 49
level crossing, Petersfield, 15, 17, 23, 41, 90 & n176, 94
Lewisham Union workhouse, 85
Liss, 90, 92n183, 93
Liverpool: *amok* incident (August 1906), 60
Locke, Ralph, 79n142
Lodge, The (cottage), Nether Wallop, 50
London Road, 5, 7, 8, 11, 13
Lord, Thomas, 47n75
Lucas, Arthur, 71
Luggar, Henry, 42n66
Luker, W & R (land agents), Petersfield, 16
Lunacy Act (1890), 94 & n192

Machray, Robert, *The Night Side of London,* 54
magistrates' court, Petersfield: built, 38; Dr Cross brought before, 37; Mitchell's committal hearing, 12, 26, 27, 38–9, 63–6; Goldsmith brought before, 91–2 & n183, 93
Malaysia: *amok* attacks, 60
Malta, 51
Martin, Minnie *see* Mitchell, Minnie
Mathews, Charles, 27n43
Maudsley, Henry, 71
McGregor, Dr James: examines Mitchell, 63; testifies at trial, 61, 74–5
Mellersh, William, 26–7
Mercier, Charles, *Criminal Responsibility,* 82
Methodist church, Station Road, 15, 28, 41n64
Middle Wallop Fighter-Bomber station, 50n82

military cycling, 32
Millar, Frederick (possible alias of Herbert Mitchell), 52, 57
Mitchell, Albert Slade (son), 53, 79 & n141, 85, 90
Mitchell, Charles (alias of Herbert Mitchell), 53, 57
Mitchell, Charlotte (half-sister), 50
Mitchell, Doris Kathleen (*later* Carpenter) (daughter): birth, 56 & n97; in workhouse, 85; at Dillwyn Road, 79n141; schooling, 85; marriage and children, 91; death, 91
Mitchell, Elizabeth *see* Ansett, Elizabeth
Mitchell, Elizabeth (*née* Alding) (mother), 49, 50
Mitchell, Ethel Joan (daughter-in-law), 90
Mitchell, Fanny (half-sister), 50
Mitchell, Frances (half-sister), 50
Mitchell, George (half-brother), 50
Mitchell, Herbert Cyril John
EARLY LIFE: family background, 49, 50; supposed history of insanity in family, 43, 46 & n72; illegitimate birth, 50; childhood, 50–1; trains as boy signaller, 51; serves on HMS *Pyramus* (1900), 51; hospitalised in Smyrna, 51–2; returns to England, 52; possibly stays with half-sister Elizabeth, 52; marriage to Minnie Martin, 52–3; marital relations, 55, 57; birth of son Albert, 53
IN ROYAL NAVY: enlists in Royal Navy (1903), 53; trains as stoker, 54–5; drafted to HMS *Hannibal,* 55; assaults commanding officer, 55–6; court-martialed, 56; in Dorchester prison, 56; birth of daughter Doris, 56; employed as engine fitter, 56, 57; supposedly runs amok in Sydenham, 56–7 & n99; re-enlists in Royal Navy (1906), 57; schemes to get invalided from service, 58–9, 60–1; mock fight with Harry Bentley, 44–5, 58; under observation at Haslar, 45, 58, 59; discharged cured, 45, 59
SHOOTING SPREE: plans shooting spree, 59, 60–1; firearms training, 6, 54, 61; competent rifleman, 22; steals ammunition, 6, 44, 57, 61; absconds from Tipner, 4–5, 6, 44; reported missing, 5; journeys across Hampshire, 7–10; in pub with tramp, 8; with soldiers near Hogs Lodge Inn, 9; cap stolen, 9 & n15, 25; scares off soldier, 9–10; reckless behaviour, 10, 13, 22; altercation with Allan Blackman, 10; sense of destiny, 10; targets Brickfields cottages, 11, 12, 13; accosted by Goldsmith, 11–12; shoots at soldier's bicycle, 12; approaches Petersfield, 12–14; runs amok through town, 14–16, 17–18, 31; oblivious to Margaret Treble's shooting, 17, 29; passes Mountford, 30; approaches murder location, 17, 28; asks directions at corner shop, 17, 29; conflicting witness accounts and likely sequence of events, 30; encounter with Mr Fox, 17–18; marches towards Stroud, 18; stalked and brought down by Goldsmith, 18; arrested, 18–19, 37
IN CUSTODY: taken to police station, 19; injuries, 37, 41; questioned by Dr Cross, 37–8, 39, 43; feigns memory loss, 37–8, 39, 61; concocts fake history of mental illness, 58–9; misdiagnosed as epileptic maniac, 42–3, 55–6, 58–9, 61, 63, 65, 69–70, 74–5, 81; wrongly portrayed as rampage killer, 21–2; half-believes in own guilt, 61–2; first appearance before magistrates, 38–9; snubs inquest hearing, 39, 40; taken to Kingston prison, 39, 63; at Kingston, 63; indicted for wilful murder, 47; second appearance before magistrates, 63–6; defence strategy, 62, 66, 70; committed for trial, 66; escorted to Winchester prison, 66; examined by prison medical officer, 69; continues to feign fainting fits, 69; strikes prison warder, 69; tried for murder, 72–5; aggrieved at conduct of trial, 75
AT BROADMOOR: committed to Broadmoor, 76, 77; admission photographs, 77 & n139; case notes, 78–9, 81; and mystery third child, 79 & n141; life in Broadmoor, 80–8; assigned to solitary confinement, 79–80; feigns fainting fit, 81; statement on Petersfield shooting, 12, 58, 81, 97–8; altercations with other patients, 82, 83, 84; visits from wife, 84; correspondence with Ada Rankin, 85–6; petitions for release, 86–7; final years, 88; illness and death, 88; inquest, 88; buried in asylum cemetery, 88; press reports of death, 89
CHARACTERISTICS: aggression and ill-temper, 55, 56–7, 69, 81, 82, 83; appearance and descriptions, 6, 8, 21, 27, 38, 53, 57, 64, 73; compared with Henry Spurrier, 46; religious persuasion, 79 & n142; seasonal affective disorder, 52, 82, 83–4; tattoos, 53, 57; venereal infection, 57 & n102
Mitchell, James (stepfather), 49, 50
Mitchell, Minnie (*née* Martin) (wife): background, 52; marriage to Herbert, 52–3; marital relations, 55, 57; birth of son Albert, 53; second pregnancy, 55; birth of daughter Doris, 56; and mystery third child, 79 & n141; brings up family alone, 85; addresses, 56n97, 79n141, 85, 90; takes in foster children, 85; visits Herbert in Broadmoor, 84; and Herbert's death, 88; later life, 90
Mitchell, Selina (half-sister), 50
Mitchell, William (half-brother), 50
Morning Post, 77
Mountford, Charles May, 29–30, 32n53
Musketry Regulations (1905), 4

Nelson, HMS: early service, 53; propulsion, 53; converted to training ship, 53; Mitchell's first period of training (1903–04), 53, 54–5; riot by stokers (1905), 6n10; Mitchell's second period of training (1906), 57–8; assault on Bentley, 44–5, 58; Mitchell returned to active duty, 59; Mitchell throws fit, 59; musketry training at Tipner, 4; and Mitchell's disappearance, 5; rumours among recruits of planned 'shooting spree', 61
Nether Wallop, Hampshire, 49–51
Newgate prison, 71
Newmans' cottage, Dragon Street, 14
News of the World, 94

Ocean Steamships (Chadwick et al.), 53
Oddfellows: Petersfield branch, 28
Old Bailey, 70

Paddington: *amok* incident (August 1906), 60
Panckridge, Dr William, 14n28, 35
Park Prewett Mental Institution, near Basingstoke, 94, 99–100
Partridge, Ernest, 84 & n160
Passingham, Charles (and family), 52
Payne, Robert, 88
Peake Farm, East Meon, 16 &n34
Pearcey, Mary, 71
Penn, Thomas, 92–3
Pepys, Samuel, 14n28
Petersfield: location, 9; railway, 16; 'sensational shooting affair', 21; life returns to normal, 66; redevelopment, 90; *see also names of individual streets, buildings and organisations*
Petersfield Chess Club, 32 & n53, 67
Petersfield Cottage Hospital, 19, 35, 36, 39, 90
Petersfield fire brigade, 32
Petersfield magistrates' court *see* magistrates' court, Petersfield
Petersfield masonic lodge, 36 & n54
Petersfield police: warned of Mitchell's approach, 13; confront Mitchell at Forebridge, 14; pursue Mitchell, 14–15, 32, 41, 65; arrest Mitchell, 18–19, 37; unarmed, 31 & n50; flawed handling of case, 36, 37, 39; cricket match, 67; and Goldsmith case, 92; *see also names of individual officers*
Petersfield police station, 13, 19, 31n50, 37, 38
Petersfield railway station, 16, 35, 39, 63, 66, 94
picture postcard, 67 & n120
Pike, Charles, 86
police *see* Petersfield police
Portsdown and Horndean Light Railway, 7, 8
Portsdown Hill, 7
Portsea Island, 3, 5, 7, 8, 89
Portsmouth dockyard, 4, 5, 53, 55; mutiny of naval stokers (1905), 6n10
Portsmouth Evening News, 21
Portsmouth prison *see* Kingston prison
Prince George, HMS, 55
Pullman, PC George: confronts Mitchell at Forebridge, 14, 41; arrests Mitchell, 18–19
Purbrook, 7
Pyramus, HMS, 51–2 & n85

Railway Hotel and stables, Petersfield: history, 16 & n33; Albert Clarke employed at, 16, 27; shooting incident, 17, 24, 28, 33; hand grenade scare, 31; Dr Cross called to, 35; murder spot, 21, 66, 90; demolished, 90
railway station *see* Petersfield railway station
Raleigh, Sir Walter, 71
'rampage violence', 21–2 & n40; *see also amok*
Rankcorn, Miss E., 86
Rankin, Ada, 85–6
Reynolds's Newspaper, 94–5
Richards, Dr Thomas Decimus: background, 69; examines Mitchell, 69; testifies at trial, 74–5; completes case profile on Mitchell, 78–9, 80
Richards, William, 23
Richardson's dairy, Station Road, 24
Rolfe, Rev C. T., 63
Rooke-Ley, Wilfrid, 64, 65, 66
Rose, Walter, 4–5; evidence at inquest, 44
Rowlatt, Mr Justice, 93, 99
Rufus, Edwin, 16
running amok *see amok*

St John's church, West Meon, 47–8 & n75
St Laurence Roman Catholic church, Petersfield, 15
St Vincent, HMS (training ship), 51
Samuel, Herbert, 87
Searle, Percy Knight, 27n43, 39n62, 71
seasonal affective disorder, 52, 83–4
Seven Stars Inn, Stroud, 18
Seward, Captain Percy, 38
Shearman, Mr Justice, 93
Shield and Mackarness (solicitors), Petersfield, 15
signallers and signalling, 51
Silver, Edward, 49
Simon, John Allsebrook (*later* 1st Viscount Simon): background, 72; prosecutes Mitchell, 73; Home Secretary, 86; rejects Mitchell's petition for release, 87
Smart's dairy, The Causeway, 13
Smith, Samuel, 82–3 & n153, 88
Smyrna (*now* Izmir), Turkey, 51–2, 83
snap shooting, 4
Sole Farm, Steep, 31
South Downs, 9, 10, 89
Sparks' tea gardens, Portsdown Hill, 7, 10
Spotted Cow (public house), Cowplain, 8
Spurrier, Lance-Corporal Henry, 46, 70
Stamshaw, Portsea Island, 4–5, 44

Standfield, F.G., *A History of East Meon*, 14n27, 16n34, 19; research notes, 19n37
Standish, Captain William, 91
Stanton Square (No. 23), Sydenham, 56n97, 85
Station Road, Petersfield: shooting incident, 15–16, 17, 24, 25, 28–9, 33; crime scene not secured, 36; murder spot as grisly attraction, 21, 66; murder spot today, 90
steamships, 53–4, 55
Steel, Mrs (of Brickfields cottage), 13, 22
Steele, Lieutenant (of HMS *Nelson*), 38
Steep, near Petersfield, 26–7, 94–5
Stockwell, PC Charles: pursues Mitchell, 17, 41; arrests Mitchell, 18–19, 37; evidence at inquest, 41; evidence at committal hearing, 65; testifies at trial, 74
stokers, naval, 53–5 & n92; mutiny at Portsmouth dockyard (1905), 6n10
Stroud, near Petersfield, 18, 37, 67
Sun Inn, Dragon Street, 14
sunstroke, 52, 83
Sydenham, 52, 56–7 & n97, 85, 90
Sydenham Hill Road school, 85
Sydenham House, Waterlooville, 7–8

telegraphy, wireless, 51
Tew, Frederick, 67, 90
Tew, Sarah (*née* Berry), 31–2
Tew, William John: background, 31–2; lack of shooting proficiency, 32, 33; pursues Mitchell, 32–3; accidentally shoots Mrs Treble, 33; avoids scrutiny, 36; liable to be charged with capital offence, 47; wins chess prize, 67; later life and death, 90
Ticehurst, Dr Charles, 36
Times, The, 71
Tipner firing range: history and location, 3; firearms training (August 1906), 4, 6, 61; safety procedures, 5, 44; Mitchell absconds from, 4–5, 6, 44; range today, 3, 89
Tipner West, Portsea Island, 3 & n3
Toomer, Ethel, 49
Toomer, Mrs (of Nether Wallop), 50–1
Treadaway, Frederick, 70
Treble, Amelia Maud: visits Petersfield with Margaret and Ralph, 16; rushes to get help for Margaret, 17; eyewitness account of shooting, 25, 28; evidence at inquest, 40; evidence at committal hearing, 65; testifies at trial, 74
Treble, Doris May, 16, 25
Treble, Margaret (*née* Edwards): visits Petersfield with Amelia and Ralph, 16; hit by bullet, 17, 33; carried into stable yard, 17, 28; tended by Dr Cross, 35; injuries, 35, 40, 46; death, 19, 35; no autopsy ordered, 35; inquest (*see* inquest on Margaret Treble); funeral, 47–8; fades from public memory, 66
Treble, Ralph: visits Petersfield with Margaret and Amelia, 16; rushes to help Margaret, 17; eyewitness account of shooting, 26; carries Margaret into stable yard, 28; sent to fetch tourniquet, 35; evidence at inquest, 39
Treble, Robert Tucker, 16, 90
trial of Herbert Mitchell, Winchester Assizes, 72–5
Trial of Lunatics Act (1883), 75
Tucker, Thomas, 16n34

Unsworth, William Frederick, 29

Vagrancy Act (1824), 47n74
venereal disease, 57 & n102, 88
Victory, HMS, 39, 47
Vigo, Spain, 55–6
Volunteer Arms, Petersfield, 17, 41

Warren (misidentified witness), 30n49
Waterlooville, 7–8, 89
Watership Down, 10 & n16
Weekly Dispatch, 64
Wells, George Walter, 84 & n160
West Meon, 47–8
West Sussex Gazette, 92
Wexford People (newspaper), 80
Whale Island, 3, 5
Whatmore, James, 46
White, Lance-Corporal, 12 & n23, 13
Wilson, George, 41–2 & n65, 45, 59
Winchester Assizes: history, 71; Albert Clarke trial, 27; Henry Spurrier trial, 46; calendar (Winter 1906), 71–2; Herbert Mitchell trial, 72–5; Douglas Fleet Goldsmith trial, 93
Winchester Castle: Great Hall, 71, 72
Winchester prison, 66, 69, 70, 76, 93, 98
Winchester Road, Petersfield, 17–18, 33, 41, 91
Windsor, William, 44–5, 66
Windsor Racecourse, 95
Winslow, Dr Lyttleton Forbes, 71
Winton House, Petersfield, 14 & n28, 35
wireless telegraphy, 51
Wood, Evelyn, *From Midshipman to Field Marshal*, 3